17-50

COTSWOLD BARNS

COTSWOLD BARNS

TIM JORDAN

TEMPUS

For Helen, Sarah and Lucy

First published 2006

Tempus Publishing Limited
The Mill, Brimscombe Port,
Stroud, Gloucestershire, GL5 2QG
www.tempus-publishing.com

British Library Cataloguing in Publication Data.
A catalogue record for this book is available from the British Library.

ISBN 0 7524 3740 2

Typesetting and origination by Tempus Publishing Limited
Printed in Great Britain

CONTENTS

ACKNOWLEDGEMENTS

In writing this book I owe an enormous debt of gratitude to the encouragement and support of my family. The girls have long since learnt to humour their father; but especially to my wife for her amazing patience over the many days of my disappearing into the depths of the Cotswolds, returning with an excitement which cannot always be expected to be fully shared over yet another fascinating barn found! Or equally, waiting in the car (either getting steadily colder or hotter, especially if there is no cricket to listen to) while I hike across another field for a possible photograph (which looks suspiciously like the last one), only to be held in lengthy conversation on returning by a curious farmer or local resident, keen to share some further insights.

Thanks too are due in no small measure to John Steane, who at an earlier 'ideas' stage rashly offered to later read a draft and whose offer was subsequently gratefully accepted. His comments and observations were invaluable and undoubtedly improved my efforts enormously. Nevertheless, he cannot be held in any way responsible for omissions and errors which may yet remain.

To Peter Keene of Thematic Trails, for patiently trying (and succeeding) to include all of the details, and changes, I asked for in the map of the Cotswolds. My thanks are extended to all the staff at the many libraries and resource centres who enthusiastically searched for my numerous requests and particularly to Miss Greenhill, Archivist at the Society for the Protection of Ancient Buildings. The initial searches in 'her attic' set me off in the right direction at least. And to the many people I met along the way, who took time to show me things that I would otherwise never have found, to share their enthusiasm for this very special part of the countryside and its heritage, and to those who bravely took me on trust into their homes or around their property to appreciate their own enjoyment of it.

Last, but by means least, to Peter Kemmis Betty at Tempus Publishing for taking on the challenge and his many colleagues for seeing it through to fruition; I am deeply grateful.

1

THE COTSWOLDS

INTRODUCTION

In a majority of people's minds the very mention of the Cotswolds conjures up images of the quintessential English countryside with its gentle rolling hills and picturesque villages supported by a number of small market towns; all built in a mellow stone which has itself weathered gently and almost imperceptibly over the years. Images which are perpetuated in tourist brochures, on calendars and even jigsaw puzzles reflect an existence which has changed little over the centuries.

To some extent this is true; its rich history and geographical characteristics have, since the Middle Ages, created a region which offers both visitors and residents alike a perspective on the past, providing an important manifestation of our heritage. At the same time it masks a number of significant changes which have evolved steadily, often with quite subtle transformations, rather than the more abrupt ones sometimes experienced in other parts of the country. The seeming gentleness of the Cotswolds also belies many of the hardships and privations endured by large numbers of its citizens over the years where life was frequently harsh and barely above subsistence level for its various labourers.

GEOGRAPHICAL AND GEOLOGICAL BOUNDARIES

Though the precise boundaries of the Cotswolds are hard to define and not easily drawn, the region nevertheless endures as a recognisable part of the country. It lies primarily in Gloucestershire, but with fringes in Warwickshire, Oxfordshire and Wiltshire. Geologically it is a limestone plateau, its sharper western edge sloping gradually down to the Oxford clays in the east, with a distinct architectural heritage. Typically the fields are outlined by dry-stone walls and many of the villages are tucked into softly glaciated valleys. With a few exceptions the towns too are in the valleys and off the high roads. In fact most of the major roads 'miss all our choicest possessions. What, for instance, can the highway traveller from Witney to Northleach tell of the Windrush – Asthall and Swinbrook, Widford and Taynton, and even Burford?' wrote Sturge Gretton in 1914.[1] This is equally if not more true today as the A40 bisects the region, now even bypassing both Witney and Northleach. The larger cities and towns of Banbury, Bath, Bristol, Cheltenham, Gloucester and Oxford all lie on its outer edges and consequently impinge little directly.

The Cotswold edge is strewn with fossil shells deposited by the prehistoric sea that once covered the Worcestershire plain. The whole of the southern and western boundaries are rounded off by beech-wooded escarpments. The wider open spaces of the northern hills contrast with the more wooded valleys and escarpment communities of the south, similarly many of the sheltered honey-coloured villages contrast with the bleaker open expanses. Where the hills cut across the north-west corner of Oxfordshire the stone has an even deeper tint as one meets the ironstone bedrock. It is, however, perhaps the single element of the local limestone which unites the entire area.

Its precise geographical limits are also not easily defined, and have even occasionally been stretched to include the entire limestone belt outlined opposite that runs from Dorset north-east to Lincolnshire (1). The formation of this belt is at its widest and reaches its highest levels, and arguably its most attractive and distinctive character, in the upland country we call the Cotswolds; essentially an inverted pear shape, some 60 miles or so in length and a little more than 30 miles at its widest. Approximately half of the land lies between 400–600ft, and the rest mostly between 600–900ft forming a scarp at the northern and western edges, with a few heights of over a 1000ft.

A more general agreement might therefore be considered to be one provided by Sutton and Hudson,[2] described as being loosely bounded by Wooton-under-edge to Badminton in the south-west, Cricklade to Lechlade in the south-east, Chipping Norton to Chipping Campden in the north-east and Gloucester to Broadway in the north-west. Such a boundary must still be considered to be

1 The limestone
belt from Dorset to
Lincolnshire with
the Cotswolds inset

fairly flexible, especially in the context of its major barns. An outline map of such an area is provided where, on the outer edges of this approximate boundary can be seen at least half a dozen of the earliest and largest barns still standing (*2*). These huge medieval barns, built with the local stone, were key features in their communities' lives. It is this slightly extended boundary which the present author has used as a framework for this book.

THE FARMING COMMUNITIES

In Shakespeare's time this region had already become well established as sheep country and the centre of England's wool industry, and much of the present-day Cotswolds reflect various aspects of this from both the natural and man-made environment. It seems a reasonable assumption too that the name 'Cotswold' derives from the old Saxon English 'cote' being a shelter, especially for animals (in this case sheep fold – as opposed to dovecote) and 'wold', a piece of open uncultivated land or bare hill. Many of the hills are still used for grazing, despite large amounts of Britain's raw wool now coming from as far afield as

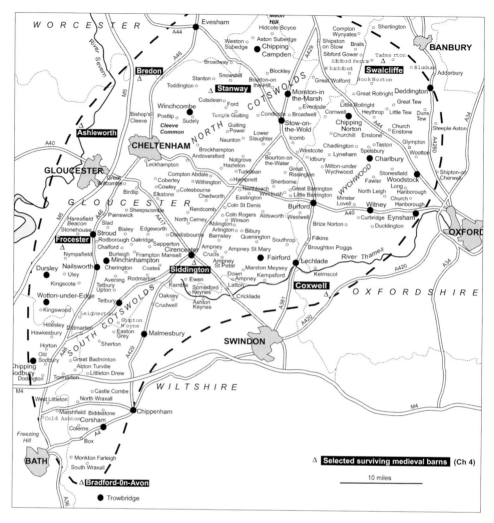

2 The Cotswolds

Australia. The rivers and streams leading into the Thames provided important transport routes for this trade, where Lechlade was also lined with old wharves which once catered for barges carrying stone for the construction of St Paul's Cathedral. The rich wool merchants built many of the fine churches such as St Mary's at Fairford, the largely fifteenth-century church of St Peter and St Paul at Northleach and the magnificent historical development reflected in Burford church, as well as the many smaller exquisite examples found throughout the region. The fifteenth-century misericords in the church at Ripple carry carvings depicting agricultural scenes. Typical homes of the wool merchants can be seen in the fourteenth-century buildings in the High Street of Chipping Campden, which was a principal centre of the Cotswold wool trade in the Middle Ages. Stow-on-the-Wold too (where ancient rhyme claims 'the winds blow cold') was a bustling centre of the wool industry. Its importance grew as a result of its position at the junction of several major roads. For centuries it held one of the biggest livestock markets in the country. Witney, straddling the Windrush, was long well known for its blankets and the much photographed Arlington Row in Bibury provided homes for the seventeenth-century weavers.

Until relatively recently most houses in the countryside were farmhouses of one sort or another: the medieval lord of the manor had his possessions under cultivation; the Georgian squire had his farm or land at hand; the priest his glebe; the miller with his share of the town fields was frequently a part-time farmer; even the miner or quarryman, labourer and craftsman, though cottagers, usually had a cow and a pig as a means of supplementing their otherwise fluctuating income.

The farmstead had three key elements: the farmhouse, the farm buildings which accommodated several processes (sometimes each function justifying a separate building, in others these several functions were carried out under one roof) and the farmyard – all being closely dependent on each other.

The farming communities still survive, albeit with the various attendant changes in agricultural practices which have had their influences on the structure, usages and functions of their buildings and the many hundreds of stone barns still to be found throughout the Cotswolds.

Given that the very name Cotswold is virtually synonymous with farming communities and the mellow characteristics of its indigenous stone used in walls and on roofs, it is hardly surprising that its farm buildings seem to blend so effectively with the landscape and at times almost appear to grow out of it.

Unfortunately, the vast majority of the remaining barns are now redundant and sadly many are falling into increasingly rapid disrepair. Nevertheless, they are an important part of our vernacular architecture and heritage, and their disappearance is a key issue to which we shall return in more detail, particularly in the final chapter.

BARNS IN THE LANDSCAPE

The building which we all associate with the farmstead, and which was generally the largest, is of course the barn; from the simple traditional threshing barns to the larger aisled barns which could store large quantities of the harvest. Later, as we shall see, both had to adapt to the development of machinery as well as often being modified for the use of animals.

Like barns anywhere, Cotswold barns were usually grouped around farmhouses and related buildings, though it is not uncommon to come across some splendid examples well away from the home farm, often high on a wind-swept wold or down in a more sheltered valley (3, 4).

The outer appearance of barns is generally determined more by their geography than by their date, where the local building materials and agricultural practices influence the colour and size of farm buildings more than any prevailing architectural fashion. Perhaps nowhere is this more true than in the fertile limestone regions of the Cotswolds, from the mellow honeyed stone in much of Gloucestershire (for example around Stanway), through a paler creamy-grey in the south-east, to the deeper ironstone in the north-east of the region as seen, for example, around Swalcliffe.

The great majority of today's stone barns date from the mid-1600s to 1900, though a number of older ones, as noted, do go back considerably further. Almost the only surviving barns of the early medieval period are the enormous tithe and monastic estate barns; most of them dating back to the thirteenth and fourteenth century. Whilst these are not strictly representative of the later more common farm buildings which we all recognise, they do provide a very special contribution to the heritage and grandeur of the region with their cathedral-like proportions and structure. (Chapter 4 provides a more detailed survey of these

3 Isolated field barn between Turkdean and Notgrove

4 Sheltered group of barns at Duntisbourne Leer

magnificent buildings.) It has been suggested that the dearth of barn building between these two periods may be reflecting a decline in the wool trade which had fallen off by the time of the Civil War and the series of bad harvests around 1590. It is just as likely, however, to reflect the slow growth in population between these periods which would not have placed significantly greater demands on the arable needs and crop storage already available. When the wool trade picked up again after the Civil War, it is true that a marked expansion in building took place. Certainly many fine examples of barns date from that period, reflecting a burgeoning economy and the growth of small towns.

The barn originally was one large open, undivided space, normally dominating one side of the farmyard and was one of the most important buildings on the farm and vital to the economy of the countryside. Barns may therefore provide a reflection of rising prosperity as well as the changes from nomadic to resident farming. Subsistence agriculture gradually became business investment; crops from the countryside were needed to feed people in the growing towns and not just in the local villages. Improved agriculture increased the yields making large-scale storage essential. Barns played their part in storing the harvest, providing shelter for livestock in bad weather and, of course, they were often built to store the parson's tithe.

In parts of Europe a barn is still seen as a building solely for storing cereal crops, with cattle housed separately in byres and horses in stables. Strictly speaking this is perhaps the correct definition, in that the original meaning of the word *barn* was 'storeroom for barley' – from the old Frisian *bere* for barley and *erm* for a storage place. However, as we shall see, these buildings have frequently been adapted and altered to meet changing demands made upon them and we shall keep to the more general consideration of them as being a multifunctional building.

Generally they were relatively large buildings, usually with several bays and sometimes with aisles too. Typically they were positioned to the north and east of the farm buildings to provide some protection for the yard. The barn itself was often built on an east–west axis. Its basic design seems to have remained essentially the same throughout the centuries with only the internal beam construction changing to any significant degree. (For details of basic construction methods and general design see Chapter 3.)

Functionally they were, as noted, primarily for storage of the harvested grain. In practice, because of this, they were also used as places of work – most notably for the initial processing of the grain crop, which was basically a two-part process. First the threshing (separating the ears from the straw) and then winnowing (separating the grain from the chaff), a topic we shall return to later. In time the wheat was stored for later sale and the oats and barley for use as cattle feed. Sometimes separate granaries were also built to store the grain harvest, as we shall also see. Barns often held hay too, especially 'field' barns which were built out in the pastures where they were more convenient to the animals, many of which may have previously had to over-winter outside. Shelter was also a feature for animals and it is difficult at times to distinguish between a smaller barn and a byre or temporary sheep fold.

Corn had, of course, been important since the Middle Ages, but when it superseded the importance of wool in the eighteenth and nineteenth centuries, barns were again built in substantial numbers. From the early 1800s they were also used for keeping equipment such as chaff cutters for the preparation of animal feed and, as already pointed out, it was generally in the barn that the threshing was carried out.

Later, they were used for storing other equipment and machinery. Indeed, it was the invention of machinery for reaping and threshing which was a key turning point in the subsequent initial decline and use of many a Cotswold stone barn. (For a more detailed historical development and usage, see Chapter 5.)

By 1900 large imports of grain from America had had their effects on the farming economy and barns ceased to be built until the 1940s, when changing agricultural practices and new materials introduced the modern era of farm buildings and the proliferation of the now familiar Dutch barns, and more recently the even larger modern edifices (5).

5 Modern farm buildings grouped around traditional farmhouse and barns

Barns, then, in their landscape provide an indicator of regionalism. Their shape, size, building materials, function and location all indicate a response to the locality. From them, as Fowler[3] has pointed out, we can infer tradition in architectural styles and craftsmanship, in regional and local economies and patterns of settlement and their changes over time. Like other features of the cultural landscape they did not 'just happen'. They represent a combination of forces and influences, both regional and local.

2

REGIONAL CHARACTERISTICS

The Cotswolds, as we have already noted, form the highest part of the limestone belt, though rarely rising beyond 900ft they vary between wind-swept open wolds to gentle and sometimes steeply wooded valleys. The hills reflect an almost timeless cooperation between man and nature, with this relationship determining much of the appearance of the landscape. Beech trees which provide windbreaks for exposed farmsteads, villages and the occasional barn have been utilised since Roman times. Fields are still divided by low dry-stone walls wandering over the undulating hills and covered in silver/grey, brown or yellow lichens. Distant buildings may appear a grey confusion, fitting into the hillside almost like natural outcrops of the underlying stone.

THE NATURAL WORLD OF STONE

The Cotswolds are essentially a low limestone plateau, rising gradually north-west from Oxfordshire and Wiltshire to the scarp in the west.

The unmistakable style of the Cotswold's buildings evolved in the Middle Ages from the sheer workability of the indigenous bedrock and, while subsequent styles and periods of building have had their respective influences and variations, almost all were built in the local oolitic limestone. Indeed, virtually nothing has done more towards creating the unique atmosphere of the region than the use of this stone for its buildings.

The geological formation of the Cotswolds is a relatively simple one. It consists of successive bands of clays, sands and limestones superimposed on one another. This limestone was laid down during the Jurassic period (at the time when the Jura Mountains were formed) from the bed of a shallow sea which covered the area between 130 and 180 million years ago. In these warm, sunny waters deposits of mud, pebbles, shells and fossilised material were gradually laid down. Subsequent subsidence let in more of the sea, and under the accumulating weight of the sediment part of the sea-bed sank still further so that near Northleach the lowest beds of the Jurassic formation lie some thousand feet below the surface, whereas only a few miles away they appear on the surface in the Windrush valley and in the Stour and Evenlode valleys. The lower beds of the Cotswolds belong to the Liassic series and are full of fossilised molluscs and the bones of primitive marine creatures and amphibians.

These sediments with the skeletons of numerous sea creatures were crushed together over the millennia creating the stone. Viewing it under the microscope one can see it is full of spheres of calcium carbonate crammed together rather like fish roe – hence the descriptive name of oolitic limestone where ooid means 'eggs'. In fact the paleness of the stone reflects the colour of the shells and sand as they were deposited. The variations in depth of colour are largely a product of differing amounts iron oxide. There are two basic layers, the Inferior Oolite (in whose upper and middle strata are several formations of grit named after their predominant fossils) and above this the Great Oolite (or Bathstone). Inferior here refers not to the quality of the stone, but simply to its position. Between much of these two layers lies a thick layer of distinctive clay-like rock which, when mixed with water, has the quality of *fulling* or leaching the greasy lanolin from lambswool (fullers earth).

During lower oolitic times the subtropical sea saturated with calcium carbonate formed the thickness of sediments. Uplift then caused the sea-bed to break surface and much of the lower Inferior Oolite was worn away. When deposition was resumed, rocks incorporated the remains of a rich variety of marine life, forming fossiliferous splintery rocks or ragstones.

The tilt of the Cotswolds has exposed the Inferior Oolite along the western edge and northern scarp, leaving the Great Oolite at the surface from the eastern side of the hills down to the clays of the Thames valley and Oxford. Where it is close to the surface the Great Oolite produces shabby, hard, thinly-bedded stone – much of it used as we shall see for roofing material. The lias rock occurs in thin bands among the clays and was subsequently quarried for flagstones and memorial tablets. Blocks of lias were also used for the delightful clapper bridges at Bourton-on-the-Water, Eastleach and Lower Slaughter as well as many of the flagstone floors in both house and cottage. The marlstone of the Middle

Lias forms a terrace on the Cotswold escarpment throughout its length and determines much of the character of the Oxfordshire Cotswolds east of the Evenlode. North of Bloxham it is rich in limonite and has long been mined for iron ore where it is frequently referred to as ironstone. Above the lias comes the oolite (egg-stone or roestone to many a quarryman).

Most of the stone lies close to the surface, so that relatively little effort was required to quarry it. There was a time when almost every village in the region had access to its own small quarry, though not all of the stone is of the same quality (6).

Stone from the principal quarries was used for buildings from the Oxford colleges to St Paul's and the Houses of Parliament in London. This higher-quality grade, or freestone, is more uniform and free from fossils and was formed

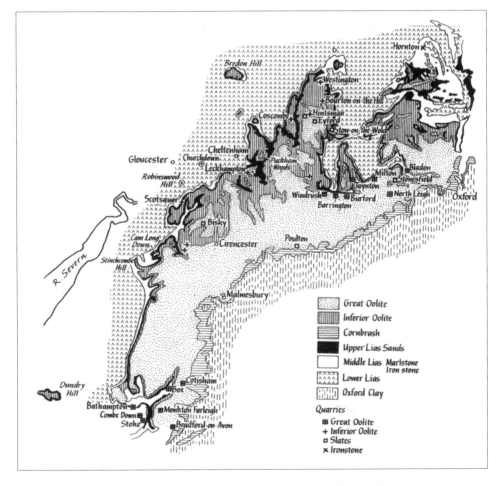

6 The geology of the Cotswolds, showing some principal quarries. *Courtesy Finberg, 1977*

in the shallower waters where there was little sea life. The Great Oolite is very fine-grained and appears in solid blocks. It is quite soft when lying beneath the soil, making it easy to shape when newly extracted. However, it hardens on exposure to the air so making it ideal as a building material. The blocks can be readily shaped and given an even surface. This is then referred to as *ashlar* when it is used to provide the smooth façade of a building or, as in the case of many of the larger barns, where it is used for quoins around doors or gables and for pillars or buttresses. Very occasionally an entire barn is built with ashlar stone, as for example at Bradford-on-Avon, Bourton-on-the Hill and Dowdeswell. Even in quite modest cottages it can also be seen carved to produce the characteristic mullioned windows. Time and wear only serve to improve its looks as the stone takes on its deeper and more varied tones, almost seeming to absorb the sun's rays on a summer day producing its familiar rich, warm evening glow. In fact it is somewhat ironical that many of the poorer cottages and barns, using the lower quality stone, have frequently weathered in more interesting ways than many of the great houses built of fine unblemished freestone blocks.

The lower grades are of additional interest to the geologist as it is in these that many of the fossils are embedded and which provide a different facet on the Cotswold's creation. It is quite possible to unearth the backbone of a belemite (a squid-like creature), or a devil's toenail (a large oyster). Digging in the muds of Cheltenham it is possible to find the bones of an ichthyosaur, a reptile which could be anything from 3–50ft long. Most common, of course, are numerous ammonites and the classic shell shapes of brachiopods found in much of the stone, especially when one is chipping away at a piece to fit into a specific niche. Many of the Cotswold's barns are built of such roughly coursed stone, or rubble-stone walling, reinforced with their ashlar buttresses at key stress points.

The layers of the Inferior Oolite cover the Cotswold plateau above the 800ft contour line. Owing to the gradual up-tilting of the area to the east, the deposits have been almost entirely worn away east of a line from Chipping Norton to Woodstock leaving just a few rare outcrops. Originally the Great Oolite probably overlay the whole of the Cotswolds, but the tilting of the entire mass left the western flank exposed to severe erosion. The Great Oolite is also recognisable from its more silver-gilt appearance when quarried.

Every town and nearly every village at one time had its own quarry and large numbers of them belong to the sixteenth and seventeenth centuries. Most would have had some freestone; the Edge especially is pock-marked with quarries. One of the better known can be found at Leckhampton where the outcrop is over 40m thick displaying a cross-section of the various bedding planes. The tower of Merton College's chapel (*c.*1310) was built from Taynton stone which also appears on most of the surviving medieval buildings in the university. It can

7 Cotswold Hill stone quarry, near Ford

also be seen at Eton, St George's chapel and Blenheim Palace. Other important quarries were at Bradford-on-Avon, Monkton Down and Corsham. Barrington and Windrush quarries also supplied stone for Windsor and the former provided stone for St Paul's and other Wren churches.

Several quarries are still in use. Coscombe quarry above Stanway has a variety of Yellow Guiting stone which weathers to a rich golden colour. Stone from Burleigh is still used for repair work on Gloucester Cathedral. The quarries around Ford (7) provide stone for a range of buildings as does the one at Farmington.

EARLY BUILDERS

The Romans built in stone too, primarily for roads and, in addition, they had two important commodities: money and masons. But the Romans had gone by AD 500. Their successors, the Saxons, where chiefly traders in timber and growers of corn and though the seventh century saw the onset of church and monastery building these were constructed largely of timber and thatch which obviously has not survived. The later Saxon period saw some abbeys and churches built in stone in a relatively simple style – and elements of this early building style can be seen in various parts of the Cotswolds, for example in the little church in Winson and the delightful tiny church at Duntisbourne Rouse where one can see 'long and short' work in the nave. At Taynton one of the oldest recorded quarries was worked by the Saxons, noted in the Doomsday Book.

The Norman lords and bishops who took over after 1066 brought with them strong stone-building traditions based on the oolitic limestone of Normandy (which is similar to that of the Cotswolds) and there followed a period of extensive building, both secular and sacred. However, it was not until some two centuries later that some of the splendid medieval barns were built which are still to be found in our region (see Chapter 4).

The mid-fourteenth century onwards saw the real onset of the Cotswolds' prosperity, based first on the wool trade and then later on the production of finished cloth. Some indication of this can be seen from the fact that Gloucester Abbey itself had a flock of over 10,000 sheep in 1300. Indeed, much of the land was owned by the monastic houses and it was claimed that the wealthy abbots frequently viewed sheep as being more important than men!

Following the Dissolution of the Monasteries during Henry VIII's reign, the masons were released from monastic and ecclesiastical tasks and were available to build private houses for the landed gentry, including farmhouses and many smaller houses in the expanding towns and villages. This period saw the rapid development of local quarries as the demand for stone grew. The Cotswolds are littered with evidence of the abundance of early quarries. A detailed look at the Guiting area alone shows numerous small quarries, most now long since hidden beneath scrub and woodland.

Arguably the greatest era of Cotswold master masons was between the seventeenth and eighteenth centuries. These men would still have worked in much the same way as the medieval mason contractors. They were in their own way architects as well as quarrymen, masons and sculptors. The Kempsters and Strongs are people one knows about and whose work is recorded in several places but there must have been hundreds, if not thousands, of other masons and quarrymen who built the fine wool churches, manor houses, barns and farmhouses. Banker masons (so called because they worked at a bank or stone bench) served an apprenticeship and were responsible for the carving of mouldings, ornaments and cornices. Each would have his own work mark which he inscribed on his work.

ASPECTS OF THE WORKABILITY OF COTSWOLD STONE

The abundant use and varied designs of finials over gable ends provides substantial evidence of the workability of the stone which is not confined to the major houses but is found on many Cotswold barns too: an exclamation at the 'end of a job well done' (see Chapter 6 for a selection of examples on barns in the region.) Some of the early finials, particularly those on some of the monastic barns, are of course thought to have had a religious significance (see for example the barn at Bradford-on-Avon in Chapter 4).

Other evidence is reflected by the frequent appearance of date-stones on the gables of both houses and barns, often with initials elegantly carved beside them. A number of these are referred to later (see Chapter 3), and one barn at Little Rollright has a second, later date-stone and set of initials side by side with an earlier one, presumably reflecting a subsequent period of alterations.

Another feature of the workable and easily-shaped Cotswold stone was the use of mushroom-shaped stones. Known as 'staddle stones', or in some places as 'dottles', they were used with planks to lift the bases of hayricks and cornstacks off the ground. They were also used to support wooden granaries, as the overlapping head of the mushroom helped prevent rodents from gaining access. (Around the area of Bisley they were also referred to as 'helms' (or hovels) and were quite common in the second half of the fourteenth century.) Most of these have long since disappeared though the original staddles can often be seen adorning many a driveway or cottage garden. The buildings themselves were generally quite basic wooden structures as, for example, the one featured overleaf at Eynsham before its demolition in 1965 (8).

8 Wooden granary on staddle stones, Eynsham: prior to demolition in 1965. *Courtesy Oxfordshire County Council photographic archive*

A few examples remain and one at Stanway (built as late as 1925 by John Oakey of Winchcombe for the author Sir James Barrie, a friend of the Wemys family) has recently been re-thatched and is now in use as a cricket pavilion.

The barns themselves, as already noted, were generally built from roughly coursed stone, though larger ones frequently had ashlar reinforced buttresses (*9,10*). The houses too, with their limestone shards, steep pitches and prominent gables have become a recognisable style of architecture, and together with the barns and farm buildings many consider 'it is in their groupings that they are most instinct with loveliness'[4] (*colour plate 5*).

The fact that they also used stone for tiling the roof, not only led to their natural blending in with the countryside, but also dictated the steeper pitches of the roof and the need for strong rafters required for their support. These steep pitches produced large roof spaces, which not only explains why their houses had so many dormers and gables but also provided a considerable storage advantage in their barns.

Above: 9 Ashlar buttresses and quoins, Doughton

Below: 10 Stone buttresses at Ablington and Coxwell

COTSWOLD STONE TILES/SLATES

The stone tiles, so ubiquitous to the Cotswolds, warrant a more detailed look at this point since they have produced not only an enduring and attractive feature seen on many of the old houses and cottages throughout the region, but they are also an equally dominant aspect of its barns and farm buildings. On small and large barns alike these roofs have, over the centuries, provided an integral contribution to the vernacular architecture of the Cotswolds. Indeed, these oolitic slates provide some of the most beautiful roofing materials and, despite their cost in terms of digging and preparation, were found on every cottage and barn, and even more lowly pig-sties and outhouses. Owing to their greater exposure to the weather they are generally darker than the walls, but the irregularity of their edges as well as their graduated sizes provide a richness of texture which many believe is unsurpassed. Together they make so many of the small village clusters seem to fit so snugly into the surrounding countryside. They have also had a significant impact not just on barn development and structure, but indirectly on their later redundancy and decay due to the expense of maintaining them in a sound condition.

While two major areas, Bath and Stonesfield near Witney in Oxfordshire, have provided much of the source materials for these roofs they were by no means the only ones (in Northamptonshire the tiles are known as Collywestons). Nevertheless, over a substantial part of the region these are now frequently referred to by the generic term of 'Stonesfield Slate'. This has had a tendency to lead to a number of misconceptions by the population in general, both local and more distant.

The term 'slates', as applied to these products of the Cotswolds, is somewhat of a misnomer too, since geologically they have nothing to do with slate as such. An alternative term, stone tiles, may not be a more accurate description either, since tiles are generally made from clay and are not quarried as is the raw material for these roofs. Aston (1974) claims they should really be called 'tilestone' or indeed, 'fissile flat stone'. Fissile material being material which readily splits along bedding planes. It is this characteristic which is so critical in allowing the stone to be split into comparatively thin pieces. (The use of stone slates goes back at least to Roman times when their occupation of the Cotswolds was widespread. It is also known that they were produced in the Guiting and Eynford areas in the twelfth and thirteenth centuries.) At Stonesfield the quarries were opened in the sixteenth century where the known slate-bearing beds occupied only a relatively small area of some 2–2.5 miles on an east–west axis to 1 mile north–south, though the mine shafts often went to a considerable depth.

Stonesfield, as noted, was only one of a number of places throughout the Cotswolds and North Oxfordshire which produced fissile stone slates, where they were generally referred to as 'slats'. The main differentiating factor of Stonesfield tiles was that they were split by the action of frost. This method left the stone (once mined) exposed during the winter in order that the moisture in the thin files of clay between the layers would freeze, expand and thus split the pendle into a manageable thickness along the natural fault lines; the frost shaling them into the thinness necessary for tiling. The pendles may also have been covered with earth or sacking to retain the moisture until splitting occurred. The force of even a single sudden thaw following a hard frost could achieve in a few hours what might have taken many weeks for a man to achieve by cracking the stone. In medieval times quarries were chosen where the stone split naturally, having been laid down in thin layers – leaving the slatter to shape and trim them. Unfrosted tiles (or 'presents') were certainly used in the Roman period, which is probably why it has also been claimed that the first slates were used on these buildings – since the area between the rivers Glym and Evenlode in which Stonesfield is situated has a remarkable concentration of Roman villa sites. The special frost splitting process which characterises Stonesfield Slate was probably unrecognised in fact until the sixteenth century, making the industry relatively modern. Clearly by the late eighteenth century it appears to have been fully developed and its products were being transported over a wide area of west Oxfordshire, Berkshire and Gloucestershire. It had, however, almost ceased by the late nineteenth century, though there are reports of two quarries being worked at Througham as late as 1910, and the Duke of Marlborough's mine at Spratt's Barn remained open until 1909.

Even the very name Stonesfield apparently has nothing to do with the mining of the stone. Stonesfield, it is said, derives from 'Stunta's field' – possibly, as suggested by Aston, an open area or space within the forest of Wychwood owned by one Stunta. (The latter incidentally is a Saxon name meaning foolish or dim!) The confusion with stone does not appear until the sixteenth century when the slate production was beginning.

The quarries of the Stonesfield district also yielded many fossilised creatures; vertebrate and invertebrate marine fossils, the remains of tiny primitive mammals, insects and flying reptiles, and even the giant carnivorous dinosaur magalosaurus. Fawler's surface quarry was especially rich in such remains.

There are numerous reasons as to why the industry possibly waned when it did, making the present upkeep and replacement of these roofs a very expensive and difficult business. The advent of new materials was undoubtedly a factor, and it has also been suggested that the onset of warmer winters began to make the frost splitting process less viable. The Stonesfield mines were for the most part small enterprises, engaged in fierce competition and it has been claimed that by the end of the nineteenth century they had virtually strangled each other.

It was also an extremely time consuming and labour intensive process with several stages involved in the final production of the slates. There was the initial quarrying and mining itself, employing large numbers of diggers or 'getters'. This was followed by problems of storage and seasonal frosting and finally the skilled business of shaping and finishing the slates by the 'slatters', 'crappers' and 'trimmers' as they were sometimes known.

It is clear from these processes that slat sizes would vary considerably and it was this very aspect that the slatters used to produce the characteristic features of these roofs with their diminishing courses of slates – with the largest on the lower rows or eaves (producing the deep overhang, before the provision of guttering) gradually decreasing in size towards the ridge. Slats were sorted by their size against a measuring (wippet) stick (11). This was usually home-made

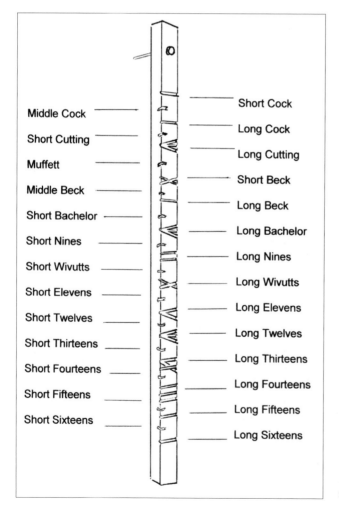

Middle Cock

Short Cutting

Muffett

Middle Beck

Short Bachelor

Short Nines

Short Wivutts

Short Elevens

Short Twelves

Short Thirteens

Short Fourteens

Short Fifteens

Short Sixteens

Short Cock

Long Cock

Long Cutting

Short Beck

Long Beck

Long Bachelor

Long Nines

Long Wivutts

Long Elevens

Long Twelves

Long Thirteens

Long Fourteens

Long Fifteens

Long Sixteens

11 'Wippet stick' or slatter's rule. *After Brill, 1973*

and marked with both vertical and slanting lines for sorting sizes and thickness of the slates. General preference was for a thickness of half an inch, though on larger expanses such as barns, three quarters of an inch was common. (Recent excavation work near Frocester has shown the sandstone tiles used by the Romans in that district also followed a graduated pattern in size from eaves to ridge – a feature not normally associated with the Romans.)[5] Typical gradations can be seen below (*12*).

Basically there were 13 size divisions, each divided into 'long' and 'short'. These sizes together with the three smallest sizes used on gables and porches (confusingly called firsts, second and thirds or teapot lids or half-teapot lids) went to make up the total number, all having delightful individual names, for example: short day, long day, long and short haghatters, jenny-why-gettest-thou or rogue-why-winkest-thou. Some of the variation in the sizes of the graduated slates can be seen from the examples in the illustration overleaf where the larger one alone measures some 80 x 50cm and weighs over 24 kilos (*13*).

The different regional sources also tended to have their own variations in names (see *Table 1*). Unusual names were not always limited to the tiles either. Pittaway, a surname curiously common in the village of Taynton at the turn of the last century (according to Sturge Gretton), is believed to have been originally

12 Typical gradations of Cotswold stone slates

Above: 13 Variations in sizes of Cotswold slates, showing wooden pegs and holes

	STONESFIELD SLATES				COTSWOLD SLATES	COLLYWESTON SLATES
6"						Even mope
6½"	All up			All up		Large mope
7"	Short Cock	1sts.	Firsts	Short Cock	Short Pricks	Even mumford
7½"	Middle Cock	2nds.	Seconds	Middle Cock	Middle Pricks	Large mumford
8"	Long Cock	3rds.	Thirds	Long Cock	Long Pricks	Even Job
8½"	Short Cutting	Short Cussems	Short Cuttings	Short Cutting	Short Cuttings	Large Job
9"	Long Cutting	Long Cussems	Long Cuttings	Long Cutting	Long Cuttings	Even Short'un
9½"	Muffity	Muffities	Muffers	Muffity	Movities	Large Short'un
10"	Short Back	Short Becks	Short Backs	Short Back	Short Becks	Even Long'un
10½"	Middle Back	Middle Becks	Middle Backs	Middle Back	Middle Becks	Large Long'un
11"	Long Back	Long Becks	Long Backs	Long Back	Long Becks	Even Short Back
11½"	Short Bachelor	Short Bachelors	Short Bachelors	Short Bachelor	Short Bachelors	Large Short Back
12"	Long Bachelor	Long Bachelors	Long Bachelors	Long Bachelor	Long Bachelors	Even Middle Back
12½"	Short Nine	Short Nines	Short-Nines	Short Nine	Short Nines	Large Middle Back
13"	Long Nine	Long Nines	Long Nines	Long Nine	Long Nines	Even Long Back
13½"	Short Wippet	Short Wivetts	Short Wivets	Short Whippet	Short Wibbuts	Large Long Back
14"	Long Wippet	Long Wivetts	Long Wivets	Long Whippet	Long Wibbuts	Bachelor
15"	Short Eleven	Short Elevens	Short Elevens	Short Eleven	Short Elevens	Wibbet
16"	Long Eleven	Long Elevens	Long Elevens	Long Eleven	Long Elevens	Twelve
17"	Short Twelve	Short Twelves	Short Twelves	Short Twelve	Short Twelves	Fourteen
18"	Long Twelve	Long Twelves	Long Twelves	Long Twelve	Long Twelves	Sixteen
		Short Thirteens	Short Thirteens		Long Thirteens	
		Long Thirteens	Long Thirteens	Long Thirteen	Long Fourteens	
19"	Short Fourteen	Short Fourteens	Short Fourteens	Short Fourteen	Long Fifteens	Eighteen
20"	Long Fourteen	Long Fourteens	Long Fourteens	Long Fourteen	Long Sixteens	In-bow
21"	Short Fifteen	Short Fifteens	Short Fifteens	Short Fifteen	Follows	Out-bow
22"	Long Fifteen	Long Fifteens	Long Fifteens	Long Fifteen	Eaves	Short ten
23"	Short Sixteen	Short Sixteens	Short Sixteens	Short Sixteen	Undereaves or Cussomes	Middle ten
24"	Long Sixteen	Long Sixteens	Long Sixteens	Long Sixteen		Long ten
	Baggeley 1968	Hughes 1965	Powell 1959	Oxford City and County Museum	Massingham 1939	Purcell 1967

Table 1 Names and sizes at Stonesfield Slates compared with Cotswold and Northamptonshire Colleyweston slates. *Aston 1974 courtesy Oxfordshire Museum Services publication no.5*

applied to some workman from the sound of his pickaxe chipping away on the stone. The tiles, he also notes, were called according to their sizes: long wivets, long bachelors, short bachelors, long, middle and shortbecks, muffities, long days and short days.

As previously suggested, stone which could be used directly as it came from the workings was called 'presents'. Presents are considered to be the most durable, but are usually somewhat more coarse-grained. They were used throughout the Middle Ages when many of the Oxford colleges seem to have obtained their 'presents' from Gloucestershire. Quarries at Stow, Guiting, Slaughter and Rissington appear in their building accounts. In fact Corpus Christi College has recently reopened a quarry near Temple Guiting and is producing new slates from pendles where the sizes range from 6–18in.

Another feature of these roofs was that they tended to have quite a steep pitch, generally of some 50 degrees; this was to avoid or minimise wind leakage and to allow for the heavy weight of the roof. The slats themselves were 'hung' from the laths by protruding wooden pegs or nails. In earlier days the pegs were often made from oak or even sheep bones. (A delightful personal account of working with stone and the making of stone slates can be found in *The Jubilee Boy*, an account of the life and recollections of George Swinford of Filkins.) A schematic of the basic arrangement and fixings can be seen below (*14*).

The slates were generally oblong but were frequently tapered or rounded towards the 'head' (the part not exposed to view) in order to reduce the weight of the roof. The wooden wall-plate was often secured in the middle of the wall, rather than at the edge of the eave, to minimise the weathering effects and rotting. An old method of water and wind-proofing underneath the slats was known as 'torching', where spaces between the pegs and laths were filled with a mixture of plaster and horsehair to keep out draughts and snow (*15*). However,

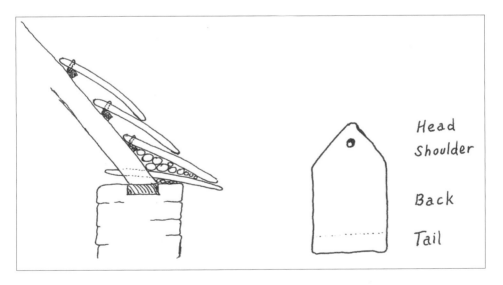

14 Arrangement and fixing of Cotswold slates

15 'Torching' in-fill on underside of slates

a problem with this was the fact that this material had a tendency to harbour damp and consequently often led to the rotting of the pegs.

Tiles are, alas, still being stripped from old barns to repair some of the older houses also in need of these materials. One barn, a mile or so from the author's own home, had one entire side of its roof (which was hidden from the nearby road) removed in a single night. This has, at least, been replaced and re-roofed with modern concrete tiles, thus preserving the essential fabric and functioning of the building, though it has lost the inherent aesthetic qualities which the irregularity of the original tiles provided. The modern tiles are also extremely slow to attract the colourful lichens, so characteristic of the traditional roofs.

OTHER (NATURAL) ROOFING MATERIALS

Another roofing material to be found, and itself requiring considerable skill and costs in terms of its upkeep, is that of thatch which was a common sight in the seventeenth century, especially in the northern Cotswolds. Though still quite widely seen in several of the Cotswold villages on their cottages and some larger houses, it is, however, a rapidly disappearing feature on barns. A thatched barn roof may cost over twice as much as a tiled roof, which is one reason why so many have been replaced with tiles.

The many styles and various techniques of thatching are well documented in a variety of sources (see for example *Thatching and Thatched Buildings* by Michael Billet) and so will not be detailed here. Nevertheless, one or two features are worth mentioning in the present context.

In many country areas thatch has been used for centuries for the protection of buildings other than inhabited dwellings. Thatched barns, for example, were commonly built, some possessing enormous thatched roofs, and a few can still be seen in the Cotswolds (*colour plates 1* and *2*). A particularly splendid one with narrow slit windows and a gabled porch entrance can be seen at Tadmarton, opposite the church. The internal roofing has arched wind-braces and is believed to date from the mid-fifteenth century. Weatherboarding, seen on the barn at Northmoor, was not used much in England before 1500. By about 1600 it was commonly being used on barns and other buildings, though much of what we see today is late Georgian in date.

Thatch itself sometimes presented a unique problem on barns in that although the roof was quite able to withstand wind pressure from the outside, if the large barn doors were left open and high winds hit the inside of the roof, then parts of the thatch were likely to lift and even be carried away. Their large size and roof areas obviously make them a very expensive item to maintain and rethatch, hence their disappearance as noted, although a few smaller barns and thatched byres are still to be found. They may also have been fewer in number in the first place in many parts of the Cotswolds. Where sheep are common there was generally less corn grown and so thatched roofs were often less in evidence. In such areas stone slates were more likely to have been used, simply due to their ready availability.

It was, of course, common practice in England to thatch ricks and hay stacks. Local specialist thatchers were rarely involved in this process as they would all have been needed at the same time – at the end of the harvest. Consequently the farm workers would often do this job, especially as the quality of the work and its durability was not so important, speed being essential. Nevertheless, many took considerable delight in the essential skills involved, even providing a decorative finial or two on the top (*16*).

The thatching of farm buildings was also generally kept relatively simple, with straight functional runs and little or no gabling or decoration. A feature also still to be seen on a few of the single storey small barns or byers was the faggot roof. Here tree branches or heavy timbers were laid across the two walls and smaller branches were then placed at right angles on these, with bundles of faggots laid

16 Rick on Woodstock Road, Witney. *Courtesy Phil Platt, Oxfordshire Museum Store*

on top of them, on to which the thatch was then pegged (*17*). This generally reflected a cheaper, less permanent aspect which may have been due to the local economy or may also relate to the agricultural depression; as such roofing could be done by the farmer or labourer, again not requiring a more skilled worker.

Most old buildings which were thatched were originally covered by materials grown in the surrounding areas – hence the widespread use of reed in Norfolk and heather or ling in parts of Scotland. Most in England now use reed or straw, especially combed wheat reed. However, in West Oxfordshire the local authority is trying to preserve the use of long straw by providing small grants for rethatching in this material. In contrast to combed wheat reed, long straw has been separated from wheat grain by itself undergoing a threshing operation which often leaves the stalks in a more tangled state. The butt ends of the long straw have not been gathered together in an orderly parallel fashion, and so it demands a somewhat different technique in its usage, and also looks different in that it is not so tightly packed. Long straw roofs are also usually finished with a decorative arrangement of spars, liggers and sometimes cross rods around the eaves and gables ends, as illustrated on p38 (*18*).

Both combed wheat reed and long straw need to be harvested using a reaper and binder – as the modern combine harvester threshes the corn as it reaps it, pouring the grain into sacks and scattering the residual straw stalks which are

17 Underside of faggot roofs at Cogges and Frocester

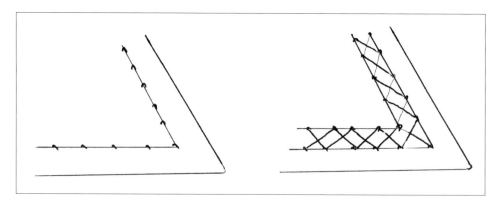

18 Long straw finishes

generally broken into small pieces. Adequate supplies of suitable length wheat straw for thatching have been further limited by the improved varieties of corn which are now grown to optimise yields. They are shorter and stiffer (to minimise wind damage) and can tolerate the higher levels of nitrogen in the fertilisers, again producing unsuitable material for thatching.

DRY-STONE WALLS

In the Cotswolds, the process of enclosure, through the latter half of the eighteenth century, produced another defining feature – that of the hundreds of miles of dry-stone walling which transformed the appearance of much of the countryside. While this had a marked long-term effect on farming practices, there were relatively few strong objections and little opposition in the countryside since it was frequently considered difficult for the weekly-wage earner to look far ahead, and enclosures afforded an immense amount of the immediate available labour needed for dry-walling.

3

GENERAL CONSTRUCTION

INTRODUCTION

Almost all Cotswold barns were built from the local oolitic limestone with their characteristic stone tile roofs. Many were built from undressed stone (or rubble) as it came from the ground, others have well defined courses of dressed or semi-dressed stone, either with or without a full mortar binding (*colour plate 3*).

Most of the old buildings incorporated lime mortars, and there would have been a kiln near every quarry. Chunks of limestone would be dropped in and heated to a minimum temperature of 880 degrees Celsius. Lime chunks would be added to water (*not* vice versa!) and after about half an hour of fizzing, boiling and bubbling lime putty would be extracted. This had a texture akin to soft cream cheese and would then be kept, under lime water in an airtight container, for a further two weeks before use. At this point sharp sand or similar would be added to make the mortar.

Cotswold barns, as we have already indicated, vary enormously in size; from the huge monastic medieval barns (averaging some 45 x 10m), large estate barns, the many hundreds of smaller ones (typically around 12 x 6m) to the more lowly field barns which began to appear in the eighteenth century.

Some of the finest barns are undoubtedly the large aisled barns, over 13m in width. As their name implies, these consist of a central nave with lower and narrower aisles, rather cathedral-like though without any clerestory; the main roof swept down over the aisles and often produced quite low eaves. The great barns at Coxwell and Bredon provide excellent examples of these. Others, such as Middle Littleton and Siddington, are partially aisled (see Chapter 4 for illustrative details). The width of the aisles would depend to some extent on the roof covering. A plain tiled or thatched roof of a steeper pitch of say 50 degrees indicates a swift steep drop between ridge and eaves, whereas a slated or stone roof with a shallower pitch of around 35 degrees would allow a reasonably higher eave line and correspondingly less wasted roof space. A number were particularly tall, and the high building of Cotswold barns (noted by Marshall in 1789) continued well into the nineteenth century. A good example can be seen at Colesbourne *(colour plate 4)*, with a date-stone of 1839, and one at Frampton Mansell is nearly 20ft to the eaves.

Most barns can clearly be seen to be divided into a number of structural and functional bays (see below), sometimes with stone pillars, but more often by timber posts. Small barns typically will have three bays, with perhaps the majority having five bays. In either case there is commonly a central 'midstrey' or 'middlestead' threshing floor with entrances on either side. Through these the horses and carts would arrive, unload the sheaves and exit through the opposite side.

Larger barns may have upwards of nine or 10 bays, in which case they normally have two pairs of doors/cart entrances and two threshing floors, though these may not always be placed symmetrically. The opposing entrance and exit doors could subsequently be left open to create a through draught which was utilised in the later threshing process (see Chapter 5 for details). In fact the large double doors were often made up of several sections so that different parts could be opened to control the draught. Later alterations to many barns have sometimes obscured the original design, though it seems clear that in a few cases the threshing floor only had doors on one side, as at Frocester. Others, such as the barn at Swalcliffe, had large cart entrances on one side and only smaller doors on the opposite side; the latter being essentially for draught purposes and not as major cart exits.

A variety of porches and protective coverings for the waiting loads are especially characteristic of Cotswold barns, and are found from the earliest surviving barns into the mid-nineteenth century. Many are gabled or hipped, sometimes quite shallowly and others are little more than external buttresses.

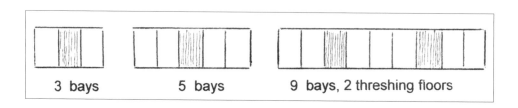

| 3 bays | 5 bays | 9 bays, 2 threshing floors |

19 Gabled porch with protective lip over cart entrance Barnsley

A typical example can be seen above (*19*). For a selection of variations on this essential style, see Chapter 6.

Occasionally there would be a porch on each side, though in most such cases it was smaller or less ostentatious in design, a good example being the ones at Middle Littleton (see Chapter 4). In others the exit doors would be simply flush with the side walls, as in the barn overleaf (*20*).

An alternative to building large barns with a number of threshing floors was to build a series of barns, sometimes for different specialities such as the wheat and barley barns at Cogges (*21*). In other instances several barns were built in a row. In such cases each would have a different plan and may have been built at different times, as for example those at College Farm in Condicote (*22*). The latter also has a peculiar feature in that the middle barn appears to have had no ground floor level access to it, either from the outside or from the adjoining barn's inner walls!

As farming practices changed, so many barns underwent substantial changes in their essential structure such as the addition of lofts, or conversions for the housing of livestock, often with additional building taking place on the outside between the gabled porches thus economising on structural costs. Such features will be considered in more detail in Chapter 5; meanwhile a typical example can be seen at Westhall Hill (*23*).

20 Simple flush cart entrance, Stanton Harcourt

21 Wheat and barley barns, Cogges, near Witney

22 Row of barns at Condicote

23 Additional building between main porch entrances at Westhall Hill

24 Field barn, near Sherbourne

The smaller, more isolated field barns, though generally built for the changing needs and uses of animals (as we shall also see in Chapter 5), often retained a single porch. In these cases it was quite commonly off-centre and only on one side, as illustrated above (*24*).

METHODS

The main methods used in the construction of barns can essentially be reduced to three fundamental types:

1. The timber-framed box or basilica type, where the walls are the essential structure and there are no internal vertical load-bearing supports. It is the walls themselves which carry the roof loads. Cross-beams were introduced to alleviate 'spreading' and consequently were wall members for this purpose. The in-fill between timber framing may be clay, wattle, brick or stone which can make an attractive decorative effect in itself (*25*). There seem to be few examples of these in the central Cotswolds, though a thatched timber-framed barn (used as a corn grinding barn), together with two others, was moved from Offenham, near Evesham, in 1927 and re-erected in Stanton; and a derelict partially-framed structure can also be seen opposite (*26, 27*).

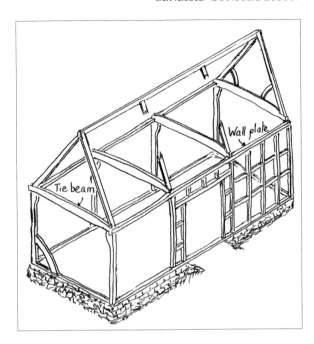

25 Box frame structure. *After Hughes, 1985*

26 Box framed barn at Stanton (removed from Offenham, near Evesham and re-erected in 1927)

27 Derelict partial box framed barn structure near Witney

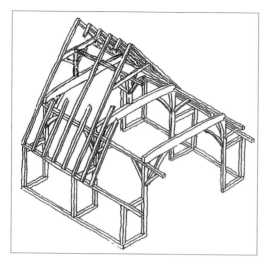

Left: 28 Post and truss construction. *After Hughes, 1985*

Above: 29 Tiebeam lap-dovetail assembly. *After Harris, 1989*

2. From the twelfth to the nineteenth century considerable use was made of the post and truss. The larger manorial buildings, in particular, would often use this more expensive framed construction where upright posts supported the roof timbers to form aisled structures (*28*). The post and truss technique was particularly suited to barn construction as the tall walls with their stout posts at bay intervals provided considerable storage capacity.

The tiebeam lap-dovetail assembly was a carpentry feature generally common to both of these structures and was in widespread use from the thirteenth to the eighteenth century (*29*). Cruck built structures were the main exception to this lap-dovetail rule.

3. The structural principle of crucks is not really different from that of the post and truss. Cruck frames were a series of large paired timbers erected at intervals as inverted Vs, or A-shaped frames. Cruck framing was one of the earliest methods used in domestic housing and it is still seen quite widely in Britain. It is also a technique found in many of the older barns and was in widespread usage from the eleventh to the sixteenth century.

The crucks are pairs of stout curved timbers from naturally curving trees having been roughly squared and split. They were then tied at the top to form an A-shaped frame. These were spaced at intervals along the barn forming the essential framework to support the walls and taking the stresses of the roof weight by means of side purlins, wall-plates and ridge poles and transmitting them to the ground via sole plates or pad stones. Supported on stone plinths, they generally went from the ground to the ridge of the roof – though some were of the raised type where the base of the cruck was seated in the side wall. Variations in cruck structures, together

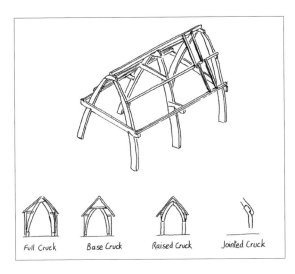

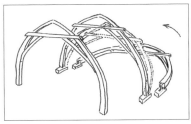

Left: 30 Typical cruck frame structure and variations

Above: 31 Schematic showing method of raising crucks

Full Cruck Base Cruck Raised Cruck Jointed Cruck

with the essential design are shown above left (*30*).

The frames would usually have been laid in their series on the ground and then raised into the vertical position as the schematic above right illustrates (*31*). (Further detail of the erection process can be seen in the drawings of Middle Littleton in Chapter 4). This made the building relatively quick and easy to erect. Their basic limitations were that they did not easily allow for sideways extension or two-storey usage. Nevertheless the array of collars and ties rarely interfered with the normal functioning of the barn.

The horizontal tiebeam would often project beyond the inclined cruck blades in order to carry the wall-plates, and the purlins were supported either directly or indirectly on the edge of the blades. In other cases the wall-plate may be placed on a tenon cut from the solid cruck blade, or on a separate wall post linked to the cruck by a spur (*32*).

The Rectorial barn at Church Enstone in Oxfordshire provides a useful example of some of these construction features, together with certain limitations which seem specific to this building. The manor and parish had belonged to the Benedictine Abbey of Winchcombe since the ninth century, and in 1382 Walter de Wynforton, the abbot of Wynchcombe, erected a barn at the request of the bailiff of the monastic grange at Enstone. This event is noted in the Latin inscription and date-stone now to be seen on the external south wall of the building:

Ista Grangia facta et fundata fuit
A.D. M CCC LXXXII per Walterum de
Wynforten abbatem de Wynchecumbe ad
Exorationem Robertii Mason ballivi loci istius

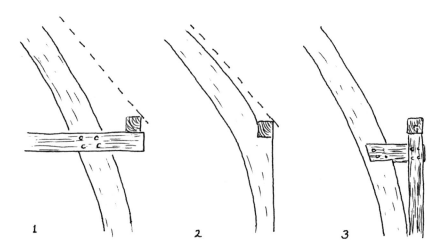

32 Variations in wall plate support in cruck construction. *After Harris, 1989* (1) On overhanging tiebeam (2) Set on attached wall (3) On attached wall post

The stone seems quite authentic, though it has clearly been reset at some point in time in its present position. It is possible that it was originally set above a stone gable. A considerable degree of reconstruction has taken place in this building over the years and in comparison with the Swalcliffe barn (see Chapter 4) and other late fourteenth-century barns in Oxfordshire and the Cotswolds this suggests that in their present form the entrance or entrances would have been under stone arches.

The barn measures some 72 x 26ft (22 x 8m) internally, with a through cartway and is divided into six bays (*33, 34*). The oak cruck blades rest in the walls, 5ft from the ground, seated on a course of large squared stones. The walls themselves rise to a total of some 12ft (3.6m). The crucks are roughly squared, showing some of the outer bark in places, and appear to be paired from the same tree-trunks. The blades are shaped, curving from the feet to knee when they then rise almost straight to the ridge. The apex is formed by a saddle, mortised and pegged to the tops of the blades. By comparison with more 'orthodox' crucks, the complete cruck being raised over halfway up the wall could be considered a regional variation, especially since it does not spring from a tiebeam, and so may represent an interim stage between a full cruck and the later truss forms. There are two collars, the lower being secured to the crucks by dovetailed halve joints, but there are no spurs extending to the cruck from the top of the wall. Nor does there appear to be a wall-plate here, and the rafters are built into the stonework at the top of the wall which is probably why extensive rebuilding and restoration of the masonry was required sometime later. There are no wind-braces either.

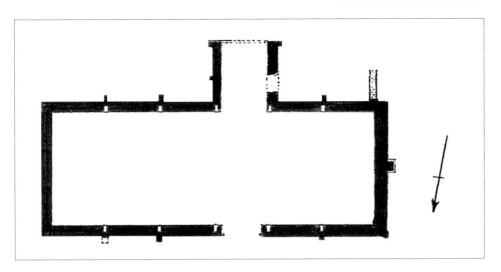

33 Plan of rectorial barn, Church Enstone

34 Interior of cruck barn, Church Enstone

Extra members, wind-braces or sway braces, were often placed in barns between the cruck blades and the purlins to provide additional rigidity. Collars, too, may be reinforced by curved braces and, as suggested, may be additionally strengthened by arched wind-braces to prevent the rafters from moving diagonally or 'raking'. In some cases, as in the tithe barns at Stanway and Middle Littleton, there may be two tiers of wind-braces (*35*).

TECHNIQUES AND DESIGN

At this point it is perhaps worth collating a schematic of the major structural components which may be identified in many of the following barns (*36*).Later barns adapted the more versatile post structure of two queen posts or a simple king post, allowing barns to be made wider (*37, 38*). There are also a number of interesting features in the various styles of carpentry used in construction. Hewett (1982) has pointed out that among the numerous subtleties (many of which have been lost to our present understanding) one or two aspects may prove recognisable to anyone seeking them out. He describes one intriguing hypothesis

35 Two tiers of wind-braces at Middle Littleton

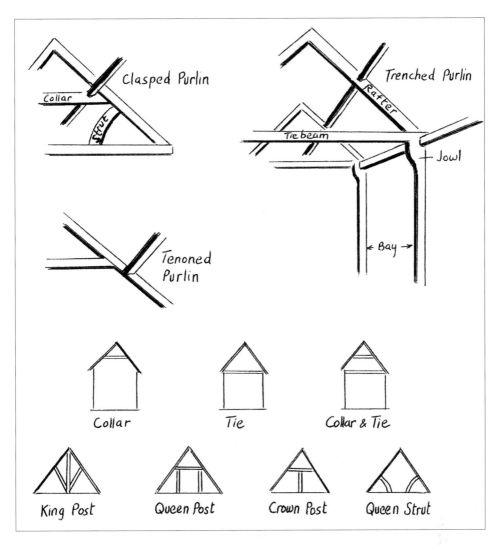

36 Major structural components found in barns

in early construction using evidence from the Barley Barn at Cressing in Essex. There it was noticed that each of the dozen great posts had plugged mortices in their feet, which lead to the speculation as to the raising of the timbers illustrated top left on p53.

The notched lap joint is another early device of carpenters – a joint which was designed to resist withdrawal. This has subsequently undergone various developments, but is essentially as shown top right on p53 and came to be referred to as Early English (*c.*1150-1250), developed with the aim of preventing the roof from spreading outward at the base.

Above: 37 Queen posts, Ashleworth

Left: 38 King posts, Didmarton

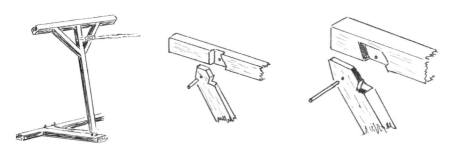

Various forms of bracing can also be discovered in the larger early Cotswold barns. The more normal assembly of the post-head joints can be seen at Bredon Barn, whereas an earlier reversed assembly has been used in the Great Barn at Coxwell. Here the tiebeam is set beneath the plate instead of being dovetailed to its top face, as illustrated below. These barns will be considered in further detail in Chapter 4.

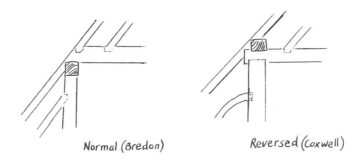

Normal (Bredon)   Reversed (Coxwell)

Crown posts were a somewhat later phenomenon. These were a single central post mounted on the centre of the tiebeams and supporting collar purlins (see *36*). They were most numerous during the medieval period; indeed, most types of roof were initially developed by the Church or monastic orders until about 1400. Toward the end of the reign of Henry VIII a *relative* decline in carpentry standards set in and men were content to build what seemed to them to be adequate, though standards were still very high by modern day comparisons and carpenters remained key people and centrally involved in the construction of barns. A selection of some typical tools used by barn builders is illustrated overleaf (*39*).

Prefabrication was of course the rule from very early times. The timber frame was often prepared in or near the forest where it was cut. Each piece to be joined to its neighbour would be numbered and then carried to the building site to be

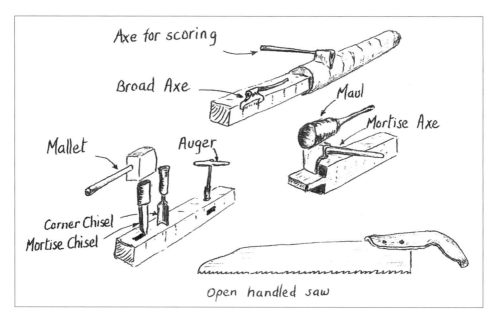

39 Selection of tools used by the barn builders. *After Steane, 2003*

reassembled. Examples of such techniques and markings will be described in the following chapter when discussing the tithe barn at Middle Littleton.

After the Reformation, the size of individual timbers in barns steadily decreased. Vertical posts became shorter and thinner. This lessening in size over the centuries became noticeable in the disappearance of the thickening at the top of the wood columns (the jowl) and its replacement by the triangular block of wood called the knee – fixed to the top of the post. Another key to dating is the scarf-joint; the joint by which long horizontal members are continued almost imperceptibly from one timber to the next (illustrated below).

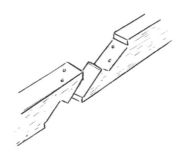

Hewett has also been able to distinguish a sequence in joint construction which allows a more detailed dating system than was previously possible. He lists the open-notched lap joint as being *c.*1200 and the hidden-notched lap joint as *c.*1250. The shorter timbers of the fourteenth century lessened the strain on joints and so gave way to the weaker feather-wedge. In the fifteenth century the edge-halved joint was preferred as were bird-mouthed bridled abutments.

Outside, wood cladding (usually elm) is a relatively later phenomenon. Horizontal weather boarding is generally seen from the sixteenth century. This, of course, requires planks of a fairly even thickness and consistency in carpentry, achieved through the use of good saws. Cleaving with axe and wedge and then squaring up with an adze was an alternative to sawing. Cleaving probably gave way to pit sawing in the production of planks when saws became more efficient.

The introduction of softwoods in the building industry around 1870 brought an obvious further change, that of machine-formed timbers. Nails too are another significant feature in the process of dating – with very few being used before the nineteenth century. Prior to that, wooden pegging was the normal means of joining timbers and these can clearly be seen in many of the older barns.

Early hand-forged nails were simply a piece of iron hammered into a nail form having a square cross-section, frequently varying in thickness throughout their length. The early 1800s saw the introduction of machine-cut nails. By 1825 heads of nails tended to be rather thin and lopsided and it was not until a further decade or so later that wire nails were invented in France. By the end of the century cut nails were in widespread production.

OTHER DESIGN FEATURES

As noted earlier the barn was frequently built on an east–west axis generally with central openings on either side. This allowed the carts to enter, unload their sheaves, and leave on the opposite side without having to turn round. The wide double doors would open on to the hard threshing floor; initially most likely an earth or gravel floor, beaten hard by years of use. Wooden floors were often added later, as these were better for threshing on as less grain tended to be lost – as long as the close boarding was well maintained. An old wooden threshing floor can still be seen at Didmarton (*40*). A number of central threshing floors were also built of stone slabs, as for example at Cogges, Swalcliffe and Lower Farm in Ramsden, though the latter has since been concreted over presumably when cattle were housed in the barn.

These basic designs seem to have changed relatively little over the centuries, with only the major beam construction changing to any marked degree. In fact even after the passing of hand flailing and threshing, 'threshing' barns continued

40 Wooden threshing floor, Didmarton

to be built for at least a further hundred years though their original function had been superseded.

Some of the eighteenth-century barns have a *columbarium* over the porch which housed the doves for the owner's table. The provision of various styles and forms of housing for doves can be seen in the gable ends of many barns and in a number of Gloucestershire's barns a granary may also be seen over a porch (*41, 42 and 43*). Additional variations may also be seen in Chapter 6 when discussing dovecotes.

Ventilation was provided in a number of different ways: often by apertures reminiscent of the narrow arrow slits found in castles (*44, 45*). Quite commonly these were augmented by a number of square or triangular holes. Indeed, some barns appear to be almost laced with these square 'putlog' holes, especially the larger barns. This is not so surprising since originally they were part of the construction process, used for the support of the scaffold poles, but were retained for ventilation purposes. Another use made of the lower square holes (typically associated with the smaller barns) was to assess and avoid the risk of self combustion from the heat generated by the newly garnered hay, or by damp in un-threshed sheaves of corn. Long metal rods would be placed through these holes, extending deep into the newly stacked hay: the rods could then be removed at intervals and felt, and if considered too warm or hot then the

41 Pigeon holes in gable end, Leighterton

42 Dovecote above porch, Ewen

43 Storage accommodation above porch, Quenington

44 Ventilation slits, Westwell

45 Ventilation slits and final exit door in side of porch, Tarlton

46 Square putlog holes,
Widford

47 Triangular ventilation
holes, near Charlbury

contents would be quickly removed (46). The triangular hole (47) is largely an
eighteenth-century development, though the reasons for these differences is not
really known.

High in the gable ends of many a Cotswold barn it is also very common to see
a smaller, often oblong, hole; perhaps conveniently provided with a protruding
'perching' ledge. These and a variety of other shapes from simple circular holes
to more complex trefoil ones, are owl holes: an ingenious provision to actively
encourage owls into the barn and thereby help in keeping down the rodent
population. These became especially apparent following a plague of rats from
Norway in the mid-eighteenth century (48).

Over the course of time, many barns have had to be re-roofed. This,
unfortunately but understandably in more recent times, has not always been with
the expensive and very heavy traditional stone tiles (the latter being too much for

Left: 48 An owl hole

Below: 49 Corrugated asbestos cement sheet roofing protecting redundant barn, near Burford

the modern slimmer rafters). Where this has been done it has at least preserved the essential fabric of the building, compared with others which have simply fallen in due to neglect and the ravages of wind and rain. Some of the materials, such as asbestos cement sheeting which appeared just before the Second World War, have begun to blend in reasonably well as a result of the weathering process (*49*). Less so some of the corrugated steel roofing: even this though, so out of place to the purist, can appear to provide some affinity with its environment at certain times of year (*50*).

50 Redundant barns with corrugated cement and steel sheeting, Little Rollright

Others have been done with the more substantial pan-tiles or, albeit plain, concrete tiles which not only protect the fabric of the buildings but also allow them still to be used either for their original purposes or more often for a marked change of function. The barn seen overleaf, with a date-stone of 1833 and re-roofed in concrete tiles, is now part of a thriving nursery (*51*).

A few have also been re-roofed, or even patched, in various types of thin blue slate which I have to say does look somewhat out of place in the Cotswold context, though may still be considered far better than leaving an open derelict shell (*52*).

DATING OF BARNS

It should be increasingly apparent from the variety of features already discussed that precise dating of many of the Cotswolds' barns is not an easy task. Nevertheless, there are a number of ways in which this can be achieved for a substantial number of cases.

1. Dating by style is perhaps the least satisfactory method, as should already be clear.

51 Replacement concrete tiles on 1833 barn near Widford

52 Blue slate tiles on small barn, Eynsham

2. Documents are obviously very useful though not always available, especially for the more humble barns. Records from the early medieval abbeys, where they still exist, have provided a valuable source (as we shall see in the next chapter). So too have college records proved particularly interesting where details have often been preserved not just of holdings but of individual costings of materials and labour charges. (See for example accounts by Munby & Steane[6] of the barn at Swalcliffe and by Dyer[7] detailing the survival of a quantity of documents from the estate records of Bredon's builders, the bishops of Worcester.)

3. Carbon-14 dating is a method that dates organic materials by measuring radioactive carbon in an object. To determine how long the object has been dead or how much C14 remains in the object a chemist must count the number of beta radiations given per minute per gram of material. The measurement of radiocarbon content thus provides a determination of the age given the known rates of decay, but it is still quite approximate compared with dendrochronological dates.

4. Dendrochronology is the study of the growth of a tree's rings in the trunk and by counting these rings one can obtain a good estimate of its age. The rings

This page and overleaf: 53 Examples of date-stones on barns across the Cotswolds

in a tree are made from xylem. (The cambium layer is the layer which keeps the xylem layer from touching the bark.) Each year in spring and summer a new layer of xylem is formed and though the rings are never quite the same, as various environmental factors alter their characteristics, the basic design is similar. A chronology of tree-rings can be built up from samples of living and standing dead trees, together with old dead wood, and this can be compared with cores taken from the timbers of a barn. There is then no way in which the barn could have been built *before* that date, though it obviously could have been at a later one, since this method provides a felling date for the timber. Confusion can of course occur if the timbers are 'second hand' having previously been used elsewhere.

5. Finally, a number of barns have actually got date-stones laid in them, generally on a gable end or over a porch; some examples are given above and on the previous page (53), and specific examples will be cited when relevant barns are described throughout the text.

1 Thatched barn, *c.*1450, Tadmarton

2 Thatched barn and stables, Northmoor

3 Variations in rubble, dressed stone, defined courses and colour on barns across the Cotswolds

4 Large barn, with 1839 date-stone, Colesbourne

5 Group of farm buildings and barn at Westwell

Above: 6 Tithe barn at Middle Littleton

Right: 7 Double tiebeams, Middle Littleton

8 External stone staircase leading to the granger's lofted lodging above the north–east wagon porch, manorial barn, Bredon

9 Granger's room with fireplace and small door at rear leading to observation balcony within the main barn, Bredon

10 Tithe barn, Bradford-on-Avon

11 Detail of timber work inside Bradford-on-Avon

Above: 12 The great barn, Coxwell

Right: 13 Cathedral–like interior, Coxwell

14 Ashlar stone barn and dovecote at Dowdeswell

15 Large barn, Ewen

16 Barn with animal shelters supported on stone pillars, near Hatherop

17 Steam threshing at Cogges Manor Farm

18 Old barn and outbuildings, Dunkirk

Opposite above: 19 Gabled dovecote and storage above cart entrance, Nympsfield

Opposite below: 20 Stone steps to lofted area above small barn, Leighterton

21 Barn at Coates, before recent conversion

22 Sett's Barn at Coates, following conversion

23 Stanway tithe barn

24 Bridal Barn, Filkins; now home to Cotswold Woollen Weavers

25 Interior of Sett's Barn, and sunset view over the fields from the threshing floor

4

EARLY MEDIEVAL ESTATE
AND TITHE BARNS

RELATIONSHIPS WITH CHURCH AND COMMUNITY

Arguably the biggest single incentive for the early building of barns was the tithe. Introduced in Anglo-Saxon times, a tithe (or tenth) of the year's produce had to be paid to the clergy as an ecclesiastical tax in support of the parish priest or rector, to help with relief for the poor and the upkeep of the church. This was stored in a tithe barn, often near the church. In practice many parishes had a rector who was not the parish priest. The rectorial duties and benefits might be in the hands of a monastery or college. Hence a monastic establishment may very well have several barns. Rectorial tithe barns were distinct from the barns or granges where an abbey or monastery would keep its own produce and which was generally larger. Over time the distinction between these has often become somewhat blurred, and the larger the barn the more likely it is that it has acquired the more generic term of 'tithe barn'. True tithe barns were primarily for the reception and storage of agricultural produce and only secondarily, if at all, for the processing of the grain crops. Either way, the Church was a dominant force for a very long time and not until the enclosure movement of the eighteenth century did it really become less powerful and the tithe system weaken. It was only when wealthier land owners had established themselves that barns, as we generally tend to think of them today, became necessary.

These large manorial and 'tithe' barns are practically the only surviving barns of the early medieval times and consequently are not entirely representative of normal farm buildings from a number of standpoints. Nevertheless, they were used for the storage of grain as well as wool and must have served as the inspiration for the smaller barns and individual farm buildings which later followed them. They were frequently enormous edifices and not completely by accident have they been described as cathedral-like structures.

The medieval Church, while urging its flock to seek their riches in heaven, was by no means averse to stockpiling its riches on earth. Looking at some of these abbey barns it is not difficult to see why the Dissolution of the Monasteries was carried out in such a relatively unhindered manner. One fine example at Stanway (as detailed later in this chapter) was built in the fourteenth century for the abbot of Tewkesbury. The town itself is some 12 miles distant, but these abbots often had vast estates. Indeed, it has been estimated that about of one third of the Cotswold region was owned by the Church before the Dissolution. Winchcombe Abbey alone had over 25,000 acres in 13 parishes.

While atypical in the above respects, a tour of these major barns which largely circle the Cotwolds will serve to illustrate many of the features which can be traced in the subsequent development of the later more familiar stone barns which are such a feature of the Cotswold landscape.

Let us begin in the north of the Cotswolds with **Middle Littleton**, which is believed to have been built in the thirteenth century. There has been some uncertainty over the origins of this barn at Middle Littleton as references in the Chronicles of Evesham state that Abbot John de Brokehampton (1282–1316)

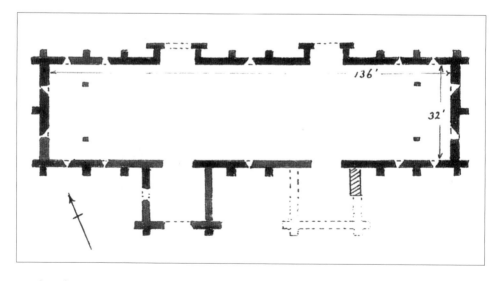

54 Plan of Middle Littleton

built a grange, 'a very fine one' at Littleton; also that a tithe barn was built by Abbot Ombersley (1367–79) at North Littleton.

In 1538 the demise of one half of a barn at Middle Littleton is mentioned, the abbey reserving 'the western end and containing five bays and a half'. This certainly refers to the present barn and recent carbon-14 tests give its approximate date as 1260 +/- 30 years. This places it well within the Brokehampton period.

It measures some 136ft (41.5m) in length, 32ft (9.8m) wide and 40ft (12.2m) to the ridge and has 11 bays, of which the two end bays are of an aisled construction (54). The remainder is a raised base cruck construction. It is built with the local blue lias limestone, the courses of which are quite regular and appear to have little in the way of any binding mortar. The sides and gables have dressed Cotswold stone buttresses at regular intervals as have the doorways and quoins and it has a Cotswold slate roof. The ends and side gables are decorated with distinctive, somewhat Viking-like, finials of which there were apparently six (below left).

Originally the building had two large wagon porches on the south side and on the north side two smaller porches, thus the main building is on an east–west axis. The two eastern porches were largely demolished, probably at the end of the nineteenth century (55, 56 and *colour plate 6*). The barn has a number of interesting features, which are discussed in the next few paragraphs.

Each of the four aisle-posts is jointed at the springing of the braces, about two thirds of the way up. The joint is a scissor-scarf, not known in any other ancient building (below right). Presumably the carpenter did not have trees of sufficient height to provide posts of a full length. This was, after all, an area already becoming a fruit (and wine) growing region.

Above: 55 Northern elevation, Middle Littleton

Left: 56 Remaining large wagon porch on south side, Middle Littleton

A complex of joints can be seen at the head of the base cruck which hold the collar beam, support the top-plate just before its jointing to the next length of top-plate, secure the top-plate with the upper tiebeam to prevent it turning or slipping outwards and support the foot of the upper principal rafter (below left).

A section at the foot of many of the crucks has been enlarged by a wedge, as shown below on the right (see also *colour plate 7*).

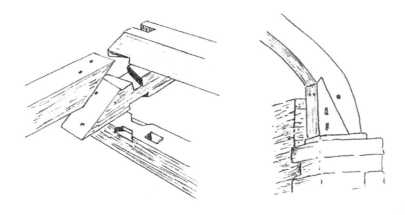

The masons, having built the west gable wall and side walls up to the level of the cruck feet, would then have to build them up to wall-head level as soon as each base cruck was raised. The wall-plate was placed at the outer edge of the walls, then the rafters set up to complete the roof structure. A schematic of how much of this was achieved can be seen in reconstruction by F.W.B. and Mary Charles (1984) where one can also clearly see the use of the putlog-holes in supporting the scaffolding (57).

Each rafter is in two lengths – from wall-plate to top-plate, and from top-plate to ridge, where the pairs of opposite rafters were half-lapped over each other and pegged.

As in all prefabrication systems, every component must be identifiable, generally by means of a number, so that each frame could be assembled by different workmen from those who put it together in the first place. The first framing and numbering would have been done at the timber yard. The numbering system is the same as that found in medieval timber buildings throughout north-western Europe. Every component of a truss bears an identical Roman numeral on its west or 'upper' face. This is the face that lies uppermost as the trusses are framed horizontally, so that it is also the face on which the pegs are driven in. The advantage of using Roman numerals was that all the lines were straight, as the carpenter's marks were scribed by a pointed instrument. Later, in the sixteenth century they were chiselled.

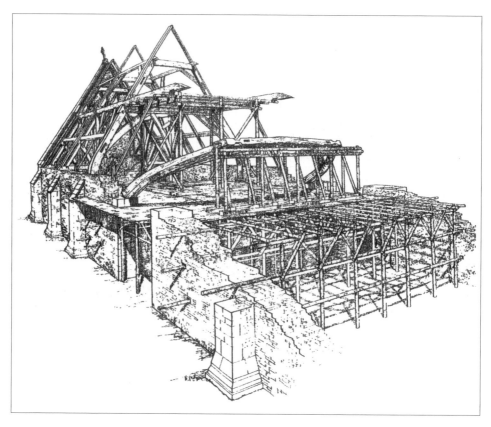

57 Method of construction and rearing of base crucks. *Courtesy Charles & Charles 1984*

Generally the numbers follow the sequence of erection, but it seems the trusses of this building must have been obtained from two sources or merchants as there are two styles of numerals. In addition, their sequence bears no relation to the order of erecting and rearing the trusses and appears somewhat chaotic compared with the usual systematic numbering seen other barns such as Stanway, Bredon and Coxwell. The numbering styles can be seen below.

Also somewhat unusual are the double tiebeams. The lower beam is, of course, essential in the framing of the arch which could not be raised without it. The upper beam corresponds to the tiebeam of the aisled frame, serving the same function as the tiebeam in any post and truss structure (*colour plate 7*).

58 Stanway tithe barn

The building itself underwent significant repairs between 1975 and 1977 following the then poor condition of the roof and some collapsing: it is currently owned by the National Trust and is open daily between 2–5pm.

Stanway, though not strictly in the 'outer circle' of the large medieval barns, is an elegant and somewhat smaller example of these early buildings. No longer a working barn, it is currently used as a village hall, theatre and community centre since its restoration in 1927 by Sir Philip Stott.

Externally it measures some 108 x 36ft (33 x 11m) with relatively low walls and a proportionately massive roof of Cotswold stone making its stone buttresses an absolutely vital part of the structure. The stone is typical of the warmer Guiting stone found in this region of the Cotswolds. As with most other villages at the time, Stanway had its own quarry, the nearby Jackdaw quarry, and the quarry at Stump Cross a mile or so up the nearby hill.

It is somewhat unusual in that it has just the one gabled central cart entrance on its north side. This has a cambered timber lintel, and a small arched stone chamfered pedestrian side door which would have been used by the granger to exit after he had secured the main doors (58). A scratch dial can also be seen on the inner face of the Jamb.

59 Roof structure, Stanway, with two tiers of wind-braces

Built *c.* 1370 for the abbot of Tewksbury, it also has striking finials above each of the gable ends and the cart entrance, reminiscent of the ones at Middle Littleton (*colour plate 23*). The magnificent sweep of the stone-slated roof is supported by base crucks set in the walls forming its seven bays. The crucks carry collars which are reinforced by curved braces and two tiers of substantial wind-braces (59).

Bredon was an important place in the eighth century when a minster or monastery there was granted a great deal of land by the king of Mercia. Its property extended from Cutsdean almost to Birmingham. Gradually, however, the estate declined and the monastery was reduced until it became little more than a wealthy parish.

The bishops of Worcester took over the land and remained lords of Bredon until 1559. These medieval bishops were extremely wealthy, holding manors scattered throughout the west midlands, drawing some £1,200 per annum (when a skilled carpenter would earn £3 a year). Bredon Barn, although traditionally known as a tithe barn (probably because the bishops were the lords of the manor for over 600 years) was, as recent research indicates, almost certainly a manorial barn. It was used for the storage of crops from the bishop's demesne and as such was quite separately administered from that of the nearby rectorial tithe barn. It stood between the manor house and the manor farm, as is clearly shown on part of an enclosure map of 1811.

It was built by the Bishop of Worcester around 1344 and measures some 132 x 44ft (40 x 13.4m) and as its width indicates it has a dramatic aisled interior with nine bays (60). Another splendid feature are the two large wagon porches on its north side (61), one of which contains a lofted lodging for the granger (*grangerius*) or reeve. This is especially rare and obviously served as an office and living quarters, reflecting the managerial resources of the organisation which planned and operated this estate. The lodging is reached by an external staircase (*colour plate 8*). It is furnished with a fireplace, the chimney of which is capped with by a decorative cowling and it also has a garderobe with a 4ft square shaft, dropping to a pit some 15ft below. The room itself has a small door at the rear which leads on to a gallery overlooking the interior of the barn from where the granger could direct the unloading of the wagons, oversee the threshing and winnowing of the grain, keep a tally of the harvest as well as keeping a wary eye out for pilfering (*colour plate 9*)!

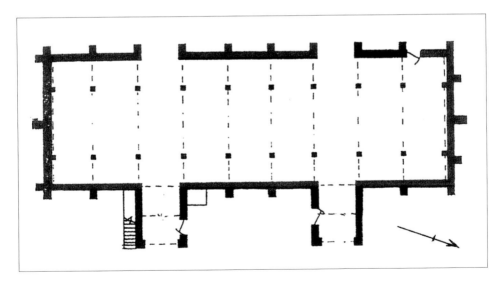

60 Plan of manorial barn, Bredon

61 Northern elevation of manorial barn, Bredon

The stonework is coursed rubble, with dressed quoins and buttresses together with the loft's chimney which has an octagonal shaft and pyramidal capping. The putlog holes in the side walls indicate that these would have been built with two stages of scaffolding; while those in the north gable would have had nine and the south seven. The latter difference presumably being due to the slope of the ground towards the nearby river.

The Cotswold stone slate roof's lower courses are approximately 3ft at the eaves, diminishing to the typical 6in at the ridge and capped by V-section stonework. Only the lower tier of the four equal height roof tiers (as defined by the purlins) has wind-braces (*62*). As a consequence of these equal lengths, the width of the nave is twice that of each aisle. The porch roofs have a similar compound rafter design, though the porch loft roof has no tiebeam, but is arch-braced. The major timbers themselves are unlikely to have been available from local woods and so would have been brought in from across the Severn, while the roofing slates came from the Guiting area.

The bishops would only visit the barn at intervals since they tended to lead a fairly itinerant life travelling between their various properties. If they stayed for any length of time, then the major function of the barn would be to store crops for the sustenance of the household: barley for malt and ale, wheat for bread and oats for the horses. At other times excess produce would have been sold and the threshed grain most likely taken to Tewkesbury.

62 Detail of roof structure, Bredon

The size of the barn also provides an indication of the social inequalities of the times as, according to Dyer,[8] there must have been around 100 peasant barns in the villages of Bredon manor in the later medieval period – none of which have survived. He also points out that the technical achievements of the barn represent the skills of its builders, the benefits derived from safe storage, and the ability to make use of both local and more distant resources, not least of which involved transporting heavy loads over considerable distances. It is persuasive that the barn's continued existence depended not only on the soundness of its initial construction, but also on the fact that it was later leased to farmers and continued to serve as a working unit rather than being broken into separate units and becoming redundant.

Sadly, the barn itself was badly damaged by fire in 1980. A number of the charred timbers can be clearly seen in the interior overleaf (*63*). Fortunately details of its original structure had been surveyed, and it has subsequently been repaired and re-roofed according to the original design. Details of its reconstruction, together with a fascinating account of how the barn was used, can be found in Charles (1997).

The entire manor at **Ashleworth** was given to the Abbey at Bristol in the mid-twelfth century by Robert FitzHardy, Earl of Berkeley and was run as a farming enterprise based at Ashleworth Court. The tithe barn was built by Abbot

63 Internal view of
Bredon, showing darkened
charred timbers resulting
from massive fire in 1980

Newland between 1481 and 1515 and is a large 10-bay barn measuring some 135 x 30ft (45.5 x 9.25m). Owned now by the National Trust it still forms part of a working farm with a piggery on its inner courtyard side. The barn itself was converted to cow housing in the late nineteenth century, presumably owing to the drop in corn prices from the late 1870s.

It has two elegant gabled cart entrances with lower and narrower corresponding doors on the opposite side. Built of the local blue lias stone it has ashlar stone buttresses at the corners, midpoint and at the corners to the cart entrances (*64*). As with many of the larger barns, Ashleworth has two threshing floors; apparently, however, it was originally two single threshing floor barns built end to end. The dividing wall was removed at some later point in time. The roof is an excellent example of queen post trusses; under the ubiquitous Cotswold stone tiles (see *37*).

Frocester Court and the surrounding lands were originally part of an ancient settlement farmed continuously throughout the Bronze Age, Iron Age and Roman periods. The current buildings occupy the site of the demesne farm of the 2,000-acre medieval manor, granted by the brother of King Beornwulf of Mercia in AD 823 to the monks of St Peter's Abbey in Gloucester. They held it until the Dissolution of the Monasteries in 1539. In 1547 Henry VIII granted the estate to Edward Seymour, Duke of Somerset. Five years later it reverted to the crown and in 1554 the demesne farm was purchased by George Huntley of Standish who built the present Court House. The Frocester estate eventually became a subsidiary holding of this estate and today the working farm comprises some 300 acres.

64 Porch and cart entrance, Ashleworth, with large split doors

The estate barn or *magna grangia de Froucestre* was built by Abbot John de Gamages sometime between 1284 and 1306 and is still in use some 700 years later. One of the longest in the country, internally it measures 186 x 30ft (56.8 x 9.9m). Rather longer and narrower than others, this too suggests a lack of suitable oak trees in the region. It is approximately 12ft to the eaves and 36ft to the ridge and has 13 bays with two wagon porches on the south side. Though some restoration work has taken place (see overleaf), it remains substantially as originally built (*65*).

The stone work is laid coursed rubble, approximately 3ft thick, with ashlar door jambs and quoins. The extensively buttressed walls are built of local lower limestone with some Minchinhampton Weatherstone dressings and the roof is a mixture of Cotswold stone and red sandstone tiles which has a hundred courses graduating from 26in at the eaves to 6in at the ridge. The entire present farm (house, stone barns and byres) was re-roofed in Cotswold stone over a period of eight years by the present owner.

Between the two wagon porches are three flying buttresses, added in the nineteenth century to provide support to the wall which had settled badly out of true. These have been roofed over and currently provide shelter as pig pens with metal doors (*66*). Other later additions include the loft doorway in the western gable, inserted windows and three nineteenth-century arched doorways, two to the left-hand side of the westernmost gabled cart entrance and one in the otherwise plain northern wall at bay 10 (*67*).

Inside is a massive oak roof, believed to have been replaced around 1540 (confirmed by radiocarbon analysis and subsequent dendrochronology)

65 Southern elevation, Frocester estate barn

66 Northern elevation, Frocester, with flying buttresses covered over and used as pig pens

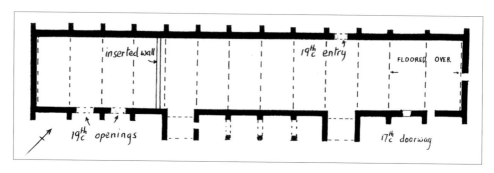

67 Plan of Frocester estate barn

 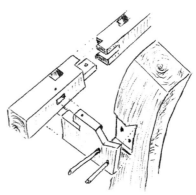

68 Roof timber structure detail, Frocester

following a substantial earlier fire which had gutted the building (*68*). The heat was so intense that the flooring was baked to a depth of 2in and there is still evidence of staining above the eastern gable window slits. A variety of structural details from 'pegging', numbering system of trusses to sequence of jointings in wall-plate and purlins indicate that the crucks were not raised in the more usual fashion, but erected piece by piece as the walls had already been constructed. This of course is consistent with the replacing of the roof (albeit to the original design) following the fire.

The trusses are formed by raised base crucks, solidly embedded in the walls, each with a braced collar beam with lighter collars above and in the middle of each bay. The wall-plate is suspended from the crucks by cruck spurs (above right).

All but one of the purlins cover two bays and the rafters which are generally 6 x 5in are in two lengths from wall to ridge. The roof also has two tiers of curved wind-braces, as seen above on the left.

Sometime following Huntley's purchase of Frocester, upper floors were inserted in bays 12–13 at the eastern end of the barn. The west end has also been given a flooring at the level of the cruck-blade bases and a further floor at wall-head level. The walls between these two levels were plastered and therefore possibly inhabited for a period. Indeed, between the top and next lowest collar, a restricted sleeping space seems to have been in use too, as the roof slopes were also plastered. The provision of doors and windows in the east end suggest similar usage was made there, though there is no indication of sleeping quarters above the top purlin. The gable windows presumably were to give light to the upper storage areas.

The final round of major alterations were apparently made some time between 1845 and 1859 when two entrances were made in bays 2 and 3 of the south wall (see earlier plan). This was done in the period Gothic style with flat, pointed arches.

At the southernmost tip of what is generally considered the Cotswolds is the magnificent tithe barn at **Bradford-on-Avon**. The Royal Manor of Bradford was granted by King Ethelred to Shaftesbury Abbey in 1001 and the great barn was built in the mid-fourteenth century. This served Barton Farm, one of the farms of the abbey which was a Benedictine nunnery. It was built primarily to store the products of the farm, though it is quite likely that the parish tithes may also have been stored in it. Subsequent excavation work seems to indicate that the barn originally occupied one side of a courtyard, in which there was a further barn and granary.

It measures 167.5 x 30ft (51 x 9m) and is divided into fourteen bays by its timber roof trusses which are raised crucks, their feet being lodged on oak pads in the walls. In some instances the trusses are built in two tiers. They also have similar profiles up as far as the collars, but vary after that point in both length and design; this again suggests variability in available timber. All of the trusses are seated on oak pads which are bedded approximately 5ft below the wall head. Opposite each truss, on the outside wall, is a substantial series of buttresses. Bays five and 10 have porches on the north and south sides, with main gables on the north side also having corner buttresses (*69*). Somewhat less deep on the south side, the gables have large flat-headed doors under oak lintels, though nevertheless are still full width, but with no side doors.

The whole of the masonry is of coursed ashlar and is a fine example of the Cotswold limestone; this together with the quite elaborate timbering gives the barn a much more sophisticated appearance than many of the others (*colour plates 10, 11*). Almost certainly the stone came from the disused quarry at the top of the nearby hill. The roof has some 80 courses of Cotswold stone tiles and the striking feature of some rather unusual weathered finials, believed to have originally been crosses (*70*).

The barn underwent invisible repairs in the 1950s by the Ministry of Works, with new foundations under the north wall and concealed plates and bolts in a number of trusses, making it as sound as or better than it was originally.

The splendid barn at **Siddington**, though next to the Norman church was most likely to have been built before the church. It is believed to be one of the oldest surviving medieval barns in Gloucestershire and dates from the thirteenth century. The stonework of the east gable has a number of details which are characteristic

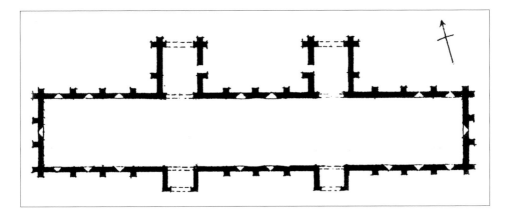

Above: 69 Plan of Bradford-on-Avon

Left: 70 Finial and gable end, Bradford-on-Avon

Below: 71 Tall split window with mid-point stone 'weatherboard', Siddington

of the Anglo-Saxon period. The tall slit window is divided at its half-way point by a horizontal stone 'weatherboard' (*71*). There is also an absence of buttresses, apart from what appear to be later additions on each side of the porch entrance. The timber work of lap joint and scissor-braces are also features of the earliest buildings and this has subsequently been confirmed by dendrochronology as dating to 1245-7. Siddington was always in lay hands, but the church passed to the Knights Hospitaller of Quenington by gift of Jordan de Clinton in about 1200.

It is a mixture of base cruck and aisled construction. Four transverse timber frames carry much of the roof. The end frames are posted and aisled, with clasping tiebeams, scissor-bracing collars and side purlins. The frames are assembled with open notched laps; all characteristic of the first half of the thirteenth century. While it now has five bays, it appears from evidence of joints in the aisle plates that the west end may originally have been longer. There is an attached smaller eighteenth-century barn and animal stables; the entire group now used as a working stables (*72, 73*). As many barns were becoming redundant with the introduction of threshing machines (see Chapter 5), a greater emphasis on cattle and a drop in the price of corn from the 1870s, some were converted to cow housing. When this happens traces are generally left on the fabric of the barn, for example whitewashing and the concreting of floors. At Siddington the tithe barn was later converted into a malting; the north porch was enlarged to form a kiln and the main barn was lofted throughout (now removed) with dormers and an outside staircase added.

The Great Barn at **Coxwell** is, as its name implies, an enormous building to the extent that it served as a landmark on its hillside above the airfield at Watchfield where even a novice pilot could not mistake it from the air.

It was a monastic grange (farm) built by the monks of Beaulieu Abbey when a cell from Beaulieu was formed at Great Coxwell following the granting of a Manor at Faringdon by King John to the Cistercian Abbey of Beaulieu, in Hampshire, in 1203. It is in fact the only surviving one of several such barns which were part of the Faringdon manor, the centre being at Wyke just north of Faringdon. Before the Dissolution, Horn (1965) estimated from his research that there were at least 2,000 Cistercian barns in England, of which Beaulieu Abbey was known to possess 27 outlying manors and granges, each with a barn.

It is therefore likely that it was completed by the middle of the thirteenth century and it remained under the direction of Beaulieu until the Dissolution when it passed into the hands of the Mores family. No monks would have lived here, but in the early days the grange would have been run by lay brothers (*conversi*) and hired servants.

The site of the barn is one of the few in the area where there is stone not far below the ground's surface, and to conform to the natural contours of the site its axis runs almost north–south instead of the more common east–west (*74*).

Externally it is some 152ft (46.4m) in length, 44ft (13.4m) wide and reaches a height of 48ft (14.6m) at its ridge. The internal measurements of 144 x 38ft provide a floor area of some 5500sq ft. It is built of roughly coursed Cotswold stone (rubble-stone walling) in which many fossil shells are still visible at the lower levels, and is reinforced by ashlar-faced buttresses and openings.

There are several slit apertures, but perhaps the more obvious features on the outside are the numerous square putlog holes in which the original masons' scaffold poles would have been placed (see schematic from Middle Littleton,

Above: 72 Siddington barn,
*c.*thirteenth century

Right: 73 Partially-aisled
structure in end bay, Siddington

Below: 74 Plan of Great Barn at
Coxwell

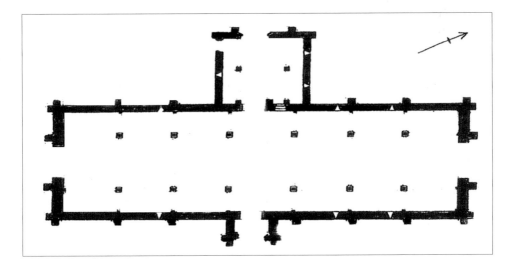

earlier in this chapter). Unlike many of the large medieval barns which we have already considered, and which have two pairs of doors, Coxwell only had one on each side (*colour plate 12*).

On the west side is a large porch and the eastern side has a smaller porch over which a dovecote can be seen (*75*). There was originally a Tallot loft in the upper part of the west porch which would have provided accommodation for the grangerius, the monk in charge of the barn. This was reached by a stair through the side door, and fragments of the boarded wall still survive. (When in the eighteenth century the west door was bricked up and the porch converted into a stable – since removed – this loft appears to have been lost.) From this vantage point both crops entering the barn and threshed grain leaving could be supervised. The roof of this porch is a miniature version of the upper tier structure of the main barn (*76*).

The only major alterations are the large doors in the gable ends which were put in during the eighteenth century, presumably to accommodate the larger wagons and loads resulting from improvements in the construction of their wheels. The roof is made of the characteristic graded Cotswold stone tiles from the Stonesfield quarry and it still has the original massive oak timbering to support them.

75 Eastern elevation, with small porch, Coxwell

76 Evidence of remains of Tallot loft in western porch, Coxwell

Being of Cistercian origin, there are certain unique carpentry aspects of design which are different from the preceding barns. The supporting timbers of the roof are of special interest in that the main load is carried by two rows of slender oak posts which were so well framed together that despite all the pressure and thrust not one has been dislodged from its original position after 700 years! These aisle posts stand on stone bases nearly 7ft in height (*colour plate 13*).

The bases are capped with oak templates, laid sideways, to prevent moisture from rising from the stone into the fibres of the posts. The posts, themselves over 22ft high, are framed together 30ft above the ground, cross-wise by tiebeams then lengthwise by roof plates. In this way they are tied back to the side walls of the aisles. This framework is strengthened at each corner by heavy bracing struts, longitudinally to the arcade plate in each direction and transversely to the tiebeam. This acts to a considerable degree in reducing the unsupported span of the tiebeam.

Each bay is designed as a square, with the same length and width, and each aisle bay a double square bisected by an intermediate principal rafter springing from the side wall. Essentially they act as braces supporting the arcade-plate.

This framework supports the rest of the roof which basically consists of a series of purlins which carry the rafters. The lower tier of purlins are trapped

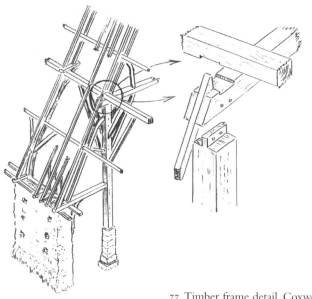

77 Timber frame detail, Coxwell. *After Horn & Born, 1965*

by a strut and secondary rafter on the main trusses, and by intermediate trusses which form a base cruck with its foot embedded in the wall. In the upper level of the roof there are two rows of purlins, the lower trapped by a secondary rafter and elbow-strut, and the upper clasped by a collar-beam against the rafter. The tiebeam is tenoned to the main posts instead of being dovetailed over the arcade plate which also makes it different from lowland aisled structures (77).

The fortunate survival of a set of fully audited accounts for 1269–70 provides an interesting picture of the running of these granges in relation to the overall economy of the abbey. Apart from wool which was collected centrally, and the requirements of individual granges for feed and seed, the entire produce was sold with the proceeds being paid in cash to the abbey. In the above accounts, Coxwell's grain production amounted to 24 per cent of the total for the Faringdon granges of that year – second only to Wyke (while only 12 per cent came from tithes). The grain was mostly wheat and oats, though rye was also important and there was a small amount of barley. It is not detailed how many of the Beaulieu flock were kept on these granges, but there is a detailed stock-list for other animals which indicates that pigs were bred at Coxwell and that there was a herd of dairy cattle too.

Coming now virtually full circle to the north-eastern tip of the Cotswolds one comes across the splendid rectorial barn of **Swalcliffe**, built between 1400 and 1409. It was part of the endowment of New College, Oxford, founded by William of Wykeham the Bishop of Winchester, and remained in the possession of New College until 1972. Wykeham was in fact the richest prelate in England

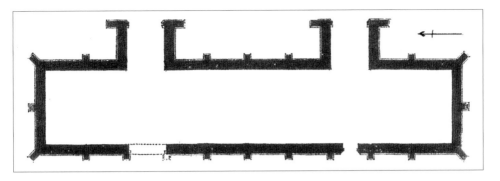

78 Plan of rectorial barn, Swalcliffe

at the time and Swalcliffe was only part of the College's endowment stretching across several counties. (There are also two other barns locally; at Upper Heyford and Adderbury.)

The College archives hold a detailed chronology of the original construction process, and apart from the creation of a further cart entrance on the south side (opposite the existing north doorway) in the nineteenth century, together with a few other minor interventions it remains substantially as it was originally built. As a result of these records and the very thorough description of its repair and refurbishment, when a sequence of investigative work was undertaken by the Oxford Archaeological Unit and the Oxfordshire Museum Service, it became one of the most completely documented barns in the region (see Munby & Steane, 1995).

It has 10 bays, defined externally by buttresses which carry the outward thrust, and measures some 128 x 23ft (39 x 7m) internally (78). It is built of the locally quarried iron-impregnated coursed brownstone rubble. The paired cruck blades average 15 x 9in at their feet and are set over 11ft from ground level, seated on large stones within the walls. The upper and lower collars are pegged to the principals with arched braces. In several places where blades of insufficient curvature at the foot apparently could not be obtained, then additional firing pieces have been pegged to them to make up the foot's profile. According to earlier descriptions of the barn, the roof also had wind-braces applied to the upper and lower purlins but these were largely removed during previous restoration. The roof itself has 61 diminishing courses chiefly of Stonesfield slates. The ridge-tiles are sawn out of blocks of Taynton stone. At each end of the eastern wall are gabled porches with high four-centred arches of two chamfered orders and there are the two small doorways with pointed arches on the western side (79, 80).

Swalcliffe provides a good example of the multi-functional uses of such medieval barns together with the various changes which have occurred over

79 Swalcliffe Barn

time. (Further details of similar changes will be considered in the following chapter.) Initially it must have provided safe housing for the basic agricultural crops of wheat, barley, peas, beans and hay – which is also a reason why the more vulnerable large wagon porches generally faced onto the more protected farmyard.

Not being aisled there were no obvious divisions which could be used to separate the different crops, though it would have been relatively easy to slot timbers into the lower putlog holes from the inside to create a divisional framework. One also assumes that the customary tasks of threshing would have taken place during the winter months.

Following the period of agricultural depression in the 1870s, when farmers could no longer compete with the vast imports of prairie-grown wheat from America, adaptation was essential. Swalcliffe's interior was whitewashed several times and lofts were inserted at either end of the barn to carry hay and cattle feed. Cattle were obviously accommodated both inside and in a single-storey shelter which had been erected outside.

In the 1950s the barn was again converted, this time to store potato and root crops, when steel beams were inserted in the central bays to support a floor. This has subsequently been removed, and following its restoration and refurbishment noted earlier, it is now used as a museum for farm machinery and agricultural vehicles, owned by the Oxfordshire Buildings Trust and leased to Oxfordshire County Museums.

80 Swalcliffe Barn, showing later additions of smaller cart entrance

COLLEGES AS LANDLORDS

Considerable portions of the Cotswolds were, and indeed still are, owned by the Colleges of Oxford. This can frequently be observed from the specific name of a farmstead, or more often by the more generic name of 'college farm'.

In many instances these were part of the original endowment of a college, or were bequeathed by a wealthy benefactor as a way of supporting the continued work of the college. Several of the older colleges have their rent rolls and bursar's accounts as well as title deeds (often dating back to the year of foundation) in their muniment rooms. In cases where there are no existing title deeds as such, they are often deemed to be part of the 'ancient estates'. Farms were also bought by the colleges themselves at a time when land ownership was a profitable investment. A working farm could provide not only a steady income but also 'payment in kind' by the provision of meat for the dining room or the making and storage of mead, as occurred at a barn at Yarnton (with a date-stone of 1716) until it became redundant. This building has recently been converted to domestic use and a photographic studio.

For a fascinating and comprehensive account of early (1350–1500) college estates and university finances the reader is recommended to consult chapter 15 by T.A.R. Evans and R.J. Faith in *The History of the University of Oxford,* Vol II (1992). College estates at this time consisted largely of their original endowment to which additions were made either by separate purchases or from later clerical benefactions. Until the early seventeenth century, Queen's College recorded its benefactors and their gifts in an obituary book.

The process of conveying properties to a college could often be a very protracted business. Land might also carry with it various obligations which could become a burden to the new owner. An important source from which late medieval foundations benefited was the English possessions of alien priories. Rural properties were generally manors which could include pastures, arable land and other assets such as barns, mills, fisheries and woods either held 'in demesne' (that is held directly by the college as lord) or through short-term tenancies. When a church was appropriated to a college the income from the parish, principally in the form of tithes, was often diverted to the college. The right to present a rector, which then fell to the college was frequently filled by a college fellow.

The upkeep of such estates provided not only a source of income to the college but also to the various labourers and craftspeople employed in their building and maintenance.

A number of these barns are still run under the ownership of a particular college, though significant numbers have been sold off over the years, thus redeeming their investment potential as other aspects of their profitability have declined. By the eighteenth century colleges would often issue a 21-year lease, though some would be as little as 11 years. Often these were kept in the same family for several generations and as long as the property was maintained in good condition, the college was generally not too fussy over what the tenant did. Changes, however, began when rents started to decline. The agricultural depression triggered some of these moves, as rents became particularly burdensome for the tenant. But it was not until the University and Colleges Estate Act in the mid- to late nineteenth century that colleges were allowed to sell off aspects of their endowments; for example when land became unproductive or when various disparate holdings could be economically rationalised. Such changes have been especially hastened by the more recent costly upkeep of barns and associated redundant buildings.

The Royal Commissioners of 1871 showed that the university possessed some 7,683 acres, and the colleges 184,764 acres: Christchurch had 30,000 acres for example and Magdalen 27,000. In 1881 Corpus Christi, one of the smallest colleges, held over 5,400 acres in the Cotswolds; this is now down to a little over 2,000 acres and many of their barns have been sold and converted to domestic housing in and around the Kineton and Temple Guiting region. The college's basic policy regarding their redundant barns is to 'engineer barn conversions, rather than letting them fall down.' Many being either useless for current agricultural purposes and/or in the 'wrong place' (see Chapter 7 for an extended discussion of these and related issues). One of Corpus's farms at Condicote, which was sold in the 1950s to the sitting tenant, is still a working farm. It has a fine set of barns along the side of the road leading into the village, one with a date-stone of 1865, and also the remains of a round-house or horse engine – a rarity in the Cotswolds.

5

HISTORICAL DEVELOPMENTS AND CHANGING PATTERNS OF USE

INTRODUCTION

An agricultural history of Britain is by necessity extensive and complex as there are substantial differences within, as well as between, regions and this is aside from the wide variety of interpretations. It is therefore not within the scope or intention of this book to attempt a further explanation. Nevertheless, any investigation of barns and farm buildings seems to demand some understanding of the farming processes for which they were intended: even if it is merely a brief prologue before the earliest of the *surviving* barns appear.

It is therefore considered worthwhile at this point to sketch in something of the origins of the Cotswolds' farming communities in order to provide a contextual appreciation of its barns, their development and later changing uses.

With the introduction of iron around 650 BC the relatively isolated peoples of the Cotswolds found themselves influenced by waves of immigrants with progressively more demanding lifestyles, despite being protected from the more aggressive coastal invasions. Prior to that they had largely consisted of expanding tribal groups which had created settlements devoted to hunting and gathering, pastoral farming and arable cultivation. This period culminated with the arrival of the Romans. Certainly with their arrival in Britain the Romans established a sophisticated system of food production, transport and storage to maintain a growing population with the development of their towns and villas. Some of their granaries were immense and their towns and villas were spread throughout the Cotswolds. They also accelerated the conversion of ancient woodland to sheep grazing downland and developed an important wool trade with mainland Europe. When their legions eventually left, around AD 400, much of this infrastructure broke down, and there followed a decline in Cotswold prosperity until the Saxons invaded – taking Bath, Gloucester and Cirencester in 577.

The Church, however, continued to assume much of the responsibility for food distribution, and bread and ale arguably became two of the most important components of the medieval diet. Monasteries also gained a reputation for charity, providing hospitality to travellers and pilgrims as well as distributing bread and alms to the poor. This was made possible by the monks who, like the Romans before them, constructed storehouses and stockpiled grain and other provisions to carry them through the lean periods.

The Saxons occupied the lowlands of England in the fifth and sixth centuries and dominated these regions over the next 500 years. They established a pattern of settlement that endured to Hanoverian times. Their settlement patterns were determined largely by the demands of their farming system; essentially they were corn growers whose lives depended on their crops of wheat, oats, barley and rye. They established themselves in forest clearings as small communities housed in little groups of steadings huddled together for mutual support, generally round a central green where animals could safely graze, and surrounded by some form of 'open-field' system. There is, however, little remaining evidence of their existence, particularly of their early period – due in no small part to the fact that they built mainly in wood.

The Normans followed, bringing a period of peace and a growing prosperity to England, making trade with the continent easier and safer, and it is really from this period that the first real influences on the design of farm buildings can be traced. A growing population demanded a steady increase in farmland, sometimes achieved by communal action or by the foundation of settlements by the king, abbot or baron, or even by a group of migrant peasants. Few farm buildings survive though to illustrate the organisation of the early medieval farmstead, as we have already noted in the previous chapter.

Bredon, however, provides a good example of these early communities using local resources, especially the good arable land by the river valleys (as well as the later confusion in distinguishing between manorial and tithe barns). It had been a thriving area from the Iron Age and into the Roman period. By the eighth century it was the site of a prominent monastery under the patronage of the king of Mercia and the normal convention was to call it a 'minster', as it was a wealthy church staffed by a group of clergy (not a community of cloistered monks). In the ninth century it came under the domination of the bishops of Worcester and was eventually divided between the two ecclesiastical organisations: the bishops (taking the major share) and the clergy, whose successors were the rectors of Bredon. The latter were also wealthy with income from the glebe and tithes. The rectorial tithe barn was attached to the rectory itself and the manorial barn stored the crops of the bishop's demesne. There would also have been scores of peasant barns in the surrounding villages alone, and similar divisions doubtless existed in other parts of the Cotswolds. Rectorial tithe barns, built to contain the produce of the glebe, though often substantial, were generally much smaller than the great monastic barns. The Cistercians alone, it has been estimated, had well over 2,000 barns throughout England – the Great Barn at Coxwell, already described, being testament to their skills and organisation.

By the thirteenth century the economic and political structure of the kingdom was beginning to revolve around the export of wool. Cotswold sheep were especially noted for their large size, long necks and depth and whiteness of the fleece. The abbot of Gloucester was shearing over 10,000 sheep and at around 1300 built the great barn at Frocester; and at Stanway an elegant and somewhat smaller barn was built, as we have seen, by the abbot of Tewkesbury. All the neighbouring abbeys from Evesham and Pershore to St Frideswide's had their sheep-walks. Virtually every parish within the wolds had downs similar to Minchinhampton Common on which peasants had the right to run their sheep. A proportion of the produce would go as dues to their landlords, and tithes to the Church – not infrequently one and the same in the Cotswolds!

Nevertheless, sheep farming was by no means the exclusive occupation of the Cotswolds' farmers. Especially on the more northern ironstone lands the main crop was corn and consequently there was a growing demand for storage in the form of barns, preferably two; one for wheat to be sold and one for the spring corn. Even in the southern Cotswolds the forest was still being pushed back to make more room for the plough.

The more important buildings were attaining a permanence by being built in stone, especially from the fourteenth century onwards. A period began which produced many fine churches, great houses and barns. One of the first surviving references of an early barn comes from an ecclesiastical estate surveying contract for a farm building in 1473. An even earlier set of records detailing costings and accounts comes from the archives of New College's construction on its Adderbury estate of a barn, a kiln, a piggery and a sheep shelter. William Mason received £20 5s 4d for making the walls of the barn with seven buttresses, John Gilkes £26 for carpentry and John Badby £6 for roofing the building with stone slates. The Swalcliffe accounts, already mentioned, go back to 1400 and detail not only the cost of building materials but also their sourcing and the provisions made for the workforce employed (see Munby & Steane, 1995).

Most of the surviving buildings of this period were, as we have already discovered, the work of the great lords of the Church and state. They were exceptional in every sense and not typical of the medieval farmstead. Nevertheless, a standard pattern in structure was becoming established in most of the barns, determined by the storage and processing needs. The two ends of the building housed the sheaves while the central area where the wagons entered provided the hard floor for threshing the grain in the winter months.

Later, substantial barns were built by wealthy laymen and merchants, but clearly reflecting the influences of the tithe and monastic barns, many with their ventilation slits – reminiscent of earlier defensive walls. Following the Dissolution of the Monasteries (1530–40) their disappearance and grip on land ownership in the Cotswolds produced a period of change and rebuilding. In many cases monastic estates passed to courtiers and county functionaries. Smallholdings and yeoman farmers began to emerge. In the more industrialised southern Cotswolds, around the Stroud and Dursley valleys, weaving settlements began to appear. These reflected the emergence of a new class of individuals and officials replacing the monks and warring barons as landowners. So the barn also reflected development and changes in both social and political power, though this was initially a slow process.

MAJOR PERIODS OF BARN BUILDING

Nationally it is estimated that some 20 per cent of barns were built between 1400 and 1700 and at least 42 per cent between 1700 and 1900 (i.e. relatively few between the early medieval barns and the major building period of the eighteenth and nineteenth centuries). Most of the Cotswold barns of today date from the mid 1600s to 1900 and various reasons have been suggested regarding the relative dearth in building between the early tithe and monastic barns and the marked increase in the seventeenth century, as we noted in Chapter 1. A particularly important contribution to the southern Cotswolds economy came from the clothiers and gentlemen of the sixteenth and early seventeenth century centred around Stroud and Bradford-on-Avon with important wool markets in Tetbury and Cirencester. A number of fine barns in this region reflect this period of wealth (*81, 82*).

Most farms would have been mixed farms (indeed the majority remained so well into the twentieth century), albeit with an individual emphasis more on crops or animals depending on their particular location. Birds were also much more important in the organisation of the early mixed farms. For a long time the dovecote was one of the most decorative as well as functional of the farmstead's

81 Large barns at Ablington (with 1727 date-stone)

82 Lowesmoor Farm, near Cherrington (1742)

buildings. In many respects these illustrated continuing feudal privilege, as the right to keep pigeons was frequently a monopoly held by the lord of the manor, or restricted to the barons and abbots, though later extended to the parish priest. It is difficult for us today to fully appreciate the significance that these birds played in the diet of medieval times. The supply of fresh meat and eggs to alleviate the monotonous winter diet was welcomed – if not always by the locals on whose grain they fed and who often saw them as an indirect form of taxation! The dovecote also held several other economic advantages too. The birds generally mated for life and were prolific breeders producing a pair of chicks approximately six times a year. This steady supply of squabs produced a softer juicy flesh compared with the older birds. In addition the by-product of a fine supply of guano was not only used as a fertiliser but was also used by the tanner to soften leather. Some splendid examples are still to be found around the Cotswolds (*83, 84* and *colour plate 14*). (A selection of their various characteristic shapes can also be seen in the next chapter.)

One did not, of course, have to build such magnificent edifices for these birds. Dovecotes were often built into the walls and gable ends of barns (*85*) (see also *41*) or the sides of the farmhouse itself (*86*) where tiers of holes can be found,

83 Dovecote and barn, Quenington

84 Barn and dovecote, Minster Lovell

often with alighting ledges for the birds which add to the intrinsic interest in the
structure and design of the buildings on which these are seen.

After the Civil War (in the mid-seventeenth century) there was a boom
in building as the Cotswold wool trade picked up once more. Many of the
great houses, farms and barns were built in the following years (*colour plate 4*).
Both landlords and tenants invested in barns built by professional carpenters.
The smaller Cotswold barns typically measured some 45 x 15ft (13.75 x 4.5m)
and sometimes incorporated timbers taken from abandoned buildings. The
steeper and remote side valleys in the Stroudwater Hills are full of farmsteads
built with considerable care and detail more commonly seen in the houses of
lesser clothiers, who in many instances engaged in sheep rearing as a subsidiary
enterprise. The wealthier individuals were also able to ride out the fluctuations
in the trade, but it was the many smaller businesses that found times could be
extremely hard. The weavers in particular were subject to volatility in hiring
and firing which frequently left them destitute for long periods of time. While
enormous political and intellectual changes were taking place over the next
century or two, agricultural practices changed relatively little and certainly
more slowly, despite the fact that the population was expanding quite rapidly. It
grew from less than 3 million in 1500 to some 5.5 million by 1700, more and

85 College Farm,
Condicote

86 Duntisbourne Leer

87 Additional building
between porches, near
Cherrington

88 Barns and stabling, Didmarton

89 Ox-house and barn (before recent conversion), Southrop (see also *141*)

more of whom were living in towns. True, there was a marked expansion of cultivated areas, with some technical developments, and ideas for labour saving were beginning to be born. The ox yolk had been superseded by improved horse collars and harnesses, to which was added the iron horseshoe, the deep plough and the horse-drawn drill.

The gradually increasing agricultural prosperity is often explained by the greater power and efficiency of the horse compared with the ox. As horses were replacing oxen as work beasts, this meant an increase in stabling needs with consequent demands on space. Aisled barns were one solution to the growing space problem where stalls could be used for both crops and fodder and in some cases for cattle too. These allowed a considerable increase in both storage capacity and differing functional uses under the same roof; though few of these are to be found in this region. Others were simply additions and extensions to existing structures seen in barns all over the Cotswolds (*87, 88* and *colour plate 15*). Small barns might also be converted for stabling and later separate stabling and even cow houses were built (*89*).

90 Granary, Ascot-under-Wychwood Manor

Grain was often stored in a purpose-built, free-standing granary, mounted as we have seen on staddlestones to protect it from vermin. A well-renovated one can be seen at Ascott-under-Wychwood (*90*). Coincidentally with the greater use of staddlestones for granaries and ricks was the invasion of the Norway black rat, which may also have encouraged the provision of owl holes seen in increasing numbers of barns from this period. These, as we noted in Chapter 3, were generally an elongated hole high up in the gable end of the barn, often with a ledge conveniently provided by the thoughtful owner – another practical way of keeping down the numbers of rats and mice (*91*).

Threshing was still an intensive time consuming process, normally done during the winter with groups of two, four or even eight men working together, especially in the bigger barns. A flail was used to separate the grain from the chaff stalks and winnowed by tossing with a wooden shovel into the draught of air created by opening the large entrance doors, thus blowing away the chaff: all requiring no small amount of skill. During the threshing process low boards or 'thresholds' were sometimes placed across the doorways to prevent the grain from spilling outside – hence the origins of the word, even if the significance of carrying the new wife over the threshold has been lost! Remnants of these boards can often be seen where the large porch doors (often protected by a canopy, cheeks or larger porch entrance) do not reach ground level, and by slots in the door jambs or door posts in which the boards were dropped to hold in

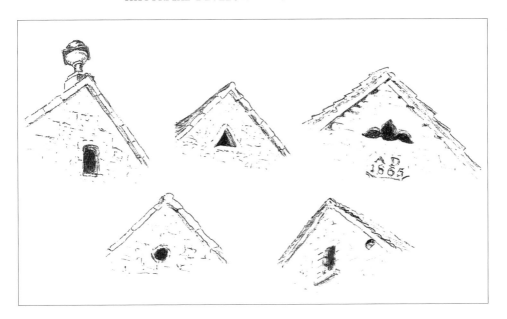

91 Owl holes

92 Doorway, Rodmarton, showing remains of 'threshold' and stone flooring

the flying grain (92). These thresholds also had the secondary use of keeping out the farmyard fowl.

Many barns had a wooden threshing floor of oak, elm or poplar. The large barn behind the church at Didmarton still has such a floor (see 40). A smooth floor was essential in order to avoid damaging the grain, and so floors would have had to be replaced at intervals when significant wearing had taken place (either by the rumble of cart wheels across them or the steady beating of flails) in order to minimise both damage and loss of grain through the gaps. Oak was generally the preferred timber, though when this was unavailable elm or poplar was used. Other barns had a stone threshing floor in the midstrey; some of these were later concreted over when adapted for housing cattle in the barn.

Hand flail threshing was a monotonous, dusty and arduous business which had to be undertaken day after day in the winter months and it has been suggested that some of the tedium of the process might have been alleviated by the keeping of a tally of the amounts done my making marks on the jamb-stones of barn doorways. If one studies these entrances closely, many have inscribed or scratched graffiti, often in the form of upright strokes or inscribed circles. Other suggestions are that some of the latter markings were intended to ward off evil spirits or ghoulies. A few examples of these tally scratchings and apotropaic markings can be seen here (93, 94).

Sheep farming was still a main enterprise on the wolds in the eighteenth century with fodder crops playing an increasingly important role on the open arable fields. (Sainfoin had been introduced as a fodder crop as early as the sixteenth century.) Some fields had already become enclosed to provide enlarged sheep flocks or improved pastures. By 1800 most parishes had undergone these transformations giving the landscape much of its present-day appearance. The

93 'Tally' scratch markings on door jambs

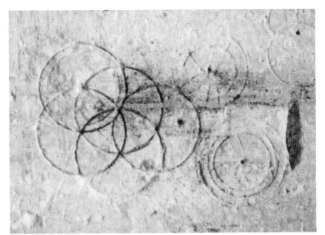

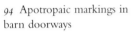

94 Apotropaic markings in barn doorways

large post-enclosure holdings were often provided with a new farmhouse and substantial farm buildings. Further significant growth in the population in the mid-eighteenth century saw landlords assembling large estates, with much of the land being leased to tenants.

As corn became more important than wool in the eighteenth and into the nineteenth centuries, barns continued to be built in significant numbers. Though still with their primary intention of being for the storage of grain, other uses were increasingly taking place. As well as the harvest, barns might also house livestock. More often cattle sheds or hovels and byres formed part of an enclosed or partly enclosed yard, bounded at right angles by the barn; these were really machines for 'manufacturing' manure before the days of chemical fertilisers (*95*, *96* and *colour plate 16*).

Left: 95 Byres and cattle housing, Rodmarton

Below and opposite: 96 Field barns with additional animal housing, near Donnington and Coates

AGRICULTURAL REVOLUTION

The agricultural revolution was a vast and rather incoherent movement which spread across the countryside over a period of some 80 years or more beginning in the mid-eighteenth century. In many areas it created the farmsteads we see today. The population was also continuing to increase. This went from some 6 million in the 1750s to 12 million by 1812. One consequence of this was the need for larger more permanent farms with better farming practices. Before enclosures, corn production had been mainly for consumption of the farmer, his family and workers. Consequently one season's harvest had to last the year as well as provide seed for the following crop, so plenty of storage was required. As arable land began to replace the sheep-walks additional building was also needed, especially when corn began to be grown on a much larger scale following enclosure. The advent of the drill to sow seeds in rows and new fodder crops began to meet some of these needs. In addition, new crop rotations demanded radical changes in open-field croppings. Though the beginning of enclosures can be traced to the sixteenth century, it was in the eighteenth century that they really gathered pace. The gradual enclosure of fields was hastened by the parliamentary enclosure movement (a large-scale formalised procedure); the main purpose of this being the replacement of the inherited strip system of open-fields. Its principal instruments were acts of parliament authorising the reallocation of land, and, physically, the boundaries dividing new farm from new farm and new fields. The outcome being essentially the pattern with which we are familiar today. In the Cotswolds, with rubble being readily available and labour cheap, this led to the rapid spread of the familiar dry-stone walls snaking over the hills.

After enclosure, acreages of barley increased and breweries appeared in Burford, Cirencester, Stroud, Deddington, Banbury, Hook Norton and Witney. The new farms created by reclamation or enclosure needed new buildings and old ones needed extension and improvement to meet the increasing demands which agricultural change was making on them. Expanded storage was also driven by the introduction of root crops and green feeding stuffs. As a result, there was considerable building and rebuilding and modification of old buildings to produce a more systematic arrangement of farm buildings according to sets of principles which gradually became widely accepted and applied in the latter half of the eighteenth century. The main criterion for this work was the implementation of a convenient layout to aid with the routine chores of feeding, littering and mucking-out.

An excellent example of these adaptations, which took place over the years as a result of the changing practices and fortunes in agriculture, can be seen at the Cogges Manor Farm Museum near Witney. (This is now a working museum, providing a history of the site where people lived for a thousand years, together with displays of old farm implements and machinery.) A schematic of

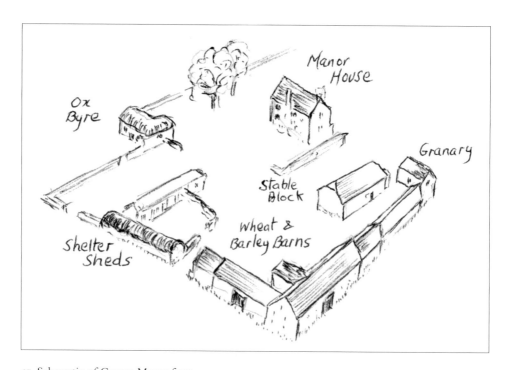

97 Schematic of Cogges Manor farm

the present-day layout is presented on the previous page (*97*). The stable block provides a good illustration of adaptation and modification over time. It was most likely built in the mid-seventeenth century as a low stone-built barn (very possibly thatched) and used as a corn barn with two large doorways facing the yard. In the eighteenth century it was converted to stabling when more heavy horses were needed to work the land, and larger barns were required for storing the grain crops (*98*). Now it is divided into two – for the working horses and a riding/hunter stabling with a typical flight of stone steps leading up to a hay loft, a stone mounting block and a small trap house at the side. (For further details see J.M. Steane ed. 1978.) The large wheat and barley barns were built sometime before 1725, reusing some of the twelfth-century stones. Both the thatched ox byre and stable sheds have the somewhat unusual 'bundle thatch' or faggot roofs – a feature we noted earlier in Chapter 2. Here bundles of twigs or faggots, bound with withies and laid over rough cross-beams, were thatched on top. This cheaper technique was one answer to the period of depression in agriculture seen from the 1870s onwards.

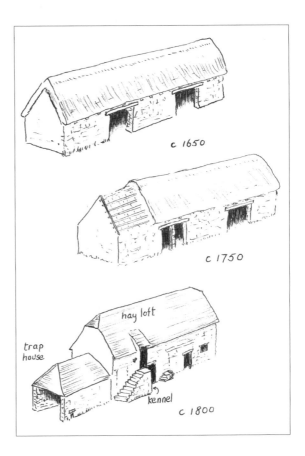

98 Sequential drawing of adaptations over time of barn and stabling at Cogges. *After John Steane, 1978*

Left: 99 Bean mill, Ewepen Barn, Sherbourne

Opposite: 100 Winnowing machine, Ewepen Barn

Adaptations and changes also took place in many of the older barns throughout the region as needs required. Lacock's fourteenth-century tithe barn initially received the rent in kind (from most of the village's inhabitants who were tenants of the abbey) of corn, hides and fleeces. Later the barn was used as a market hall, and later still it was used to store grain for a threshing machine which stood in the doorway. Ashleworth and Frocester had floors inserted at one end taking up one or two bays. At Ferris Court, Bisley, the change was more radical – the entire building being floored over for silk weaving in about 1700, only to be altered back to a barn at some later point in time.

More spectacular was the appearance of machinery on the farm. This began innocently enough in the late eighteenth century with the development of small, hand-driven machines for cutting hay and straw into chaff to reduce wastage by cattle at feeding times, for grinding corn and beans and for winnowing by a system of sails in radial arms. As the process of hand flailing was given up, dressing and winnowing machines were installed and the barn was often used as a feed store too (*99, 100*). The preparation of feed for livestock using machinery began in the 1830s and 1840s. This often required the building of a lofted section, with

the chaff cutter and cake breaker being sited on the upper floor. In 1874 Andrew Meikle (a Scottish millwright) invented a machine flail which was horse-drawn and was placed in the barn. Two years later, in 1876, he hit on the idea of building a drum filled with pegs which revolved in a concave cover and which rubbed and beat the grain off the straw as it turned (*101*).

Various modifications took place and within 20 years mechanical threshing had become established in most areas. The machine could be taken to the fields, saving considerable carting time and as outdoor mechanical threshing replaced indoor hand threshing, so the stackyard began to replace the barn as it was no longer necessary to bring the crop inside: the stack would be thatched to keep off the rain (*102*).

The barn was now rapidly losing its ancient function for the processing and storage of the corn crop, and was becoming more of a centre for the storage and processing of livestock feed. Internal dividing walls were often erected in the larger barns and, as already noted, floors inserted to provide more storage space. 'In place of the hall-like interior of the barn, the scene of great assemblies for shearing and dancing, there was now only the workshop-like interior of the mixing house with its ranks of cutting, grinding, breaking and stirring machines driven by floppy belts to the steady beat of the steam engine'.[9] Remains of some of this belt-driven machinery can still be seen in a number of Cotswold barns (*103*).

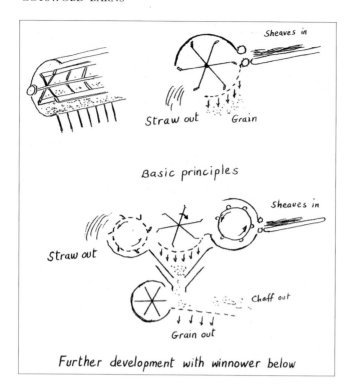

Sheaves in

Straw out   Grain

Basic principles

Sheaves in

Straw out

Chaff out

Grain out

Further development with winnower below

Left: 101 Principles and development of Meikle's threshing and winnowing machine. *After Brunskill, 1982*

Below: 102 Threshing at University Farm, Hailey. *Courtesy Corinium Museum, Cirencester*

103 Remains of belt-driven machinery in barns at Little Barrington and Oldbury-on-the-Hill

Despite all of these changes, a few 'threshing barns' continued to be built for a considerable period of time, even though their original function had been superseded. The horse was also in widespread general use by the late eighteenth century and, on several farms, was used as a means of power to drive machinery too. The horse engine, used to rotate a shaft, had long been known in the mines. Used on the farm two, four or six horses trod around in a circular path while tethered to extending poles driving a central shaft which passed into the barn. Sometimes the horse engine was located within the barn, but more often it was outside, either in the open air or in a specially constructed 'house'. The remnants of one can still be seen at College Farm in Condicote.

STEAM POWER

With the advent of steam, the whole process continued its revolution. The harvest could await the arrival of the traction engine which drove these new-fangled machines. Steam threshing had 'become common place in the last 10 years', wrote Edward Bowly of Cirencester in 1880. The machines trundled from farm to farm in the harvest season, travelling in slow lumbering convoys. They were owned by firms of specialists such as F. & W. Chew of Tetbury or John and Thomas Jefford of Moreton-in-Marsh and Chipping Norton. A fine example is still in working order and used each year at the Cogges Museum (*colour plate 17*).

Steam ploughing had also arrived during the middle years of the nineteenth century where two steam engines were used to pull a plough connected by a wire hawser to a winch and pulley. Sometimes the farmer would set the machine just *behind* the hedge (often to the annoyance of any locals passing by!) so that as little space as possible was left unploughed. Although steam ploughing died out relatively quickly, the steam engine continued to puff its versatile power deep into the fields, even in the age of petrol, turning belts for balers and pressing hay into winter feed. They were also used for the transport of limestone from the many small quarries. In fact, the Cotswolds were an area where steam-powered farm equipment was used extensively.

It was the nineteenth-century agricultural journalist Arthur Young who predicted that the mechanical thresher would 'put and end to all barn building'. This turned out to be a somewhat overly pessimistic view as the barn was once more adapted to other functions, though it is true that few *new* barns appeared after this time.

By 1900 corn production, as a single entity, had become less economic due to large imports from America where mechanisation on the prairies and reliable steam ships to transport large volumes of grain resulted in a halving of corn prices. The

Above: 104 Redundant field barn, near Burford

Below: 105 Disused barn, Coates

repeal of the Corn Laws in 1846 had already left farmers with little or no protection. This only served to keep labourers' pay low, despite the continued population growth in England and Wales. An arable agricultural depression at the beginning of the twentieth century saw barns and other buildings falling into further disuse and disrepair, especially those in the fields (*104, 105* and *colour plate 18*).

106 Windows added in gable ends for additional light, near Little Rollright and Quenington

Some barns in the farmyard itself were now only being used for housing livestock or farm implements, while others were becoming completely redundant as their doors were too small for the increasing size of machinery, or their columns too close for equipment to turn around in and the roof too low. Windows were also too small to illuminate any useful work, though some did have larger openings or windows added in the gable ends; a number of examples of this can be seen throughout the Cotswolds (*106*).

Some of the older buildings were already beginning to acquire a period charm, and although many still dominated the farmstead they were already becoming a historical relic. Roof tiles were allowed to slip and maintenance and repair in many instances was becoming prohibitively expensive.

One might argue that the tractor completed much of this process, which in the Middle Ages had taken a year and hundreds of people to complete and which now takes but a week and a large machine.

No further barn building was seen until the Second World War when agriculture underwent a marked change, together with new materials and new styles, which saw the advent of our modern buildings. Architecturally, of course, a big change came with the introduction of the Dutch barn; built with one side at least being open for the easy loading of ever increasing bulk (*107*).

107 Dutch barn, near Stow-on-the-Wold

In the years of austerity following 1945, farmers, like everyone else, had to make the best of existing resources. However, in the 1950s the Ministry of Agriculture concluded that many traditional agricultural buildings were not so much outworn as outmoded and could not be easily adapted to new techniques and machinery, to new methods of storage and handling livestock or to the new types of crops. As a result, traditional barns experienced a further redundancy as techniques changed and as farms amalgamated. The process was accelerated by the introduction of Farm Capital Grants in 1957. These provided aid with new buildings and only rarely were grants given for existing structures. New machinery and the latest combine harvesters can now only be accommodated in the very largest of buildings.

This has resulted in much of our present-day conundrum of what to do with these remaining stone buildings. Obtaining a satisfactory balance and policy for converting old barns for new uses (especially with regard to their conversions for domestic use – which more often than not changes the whole character of the building) against that of simply allowing them to fall into complete ruin with the consequent loss to much of our vernacular heritage is the challenge facing virtually every district in the Cotswolds, as well as many other parts of the country. It is some of these issues which will be taken up in the final chapter.

6

MISCELLANY

Not every interesting aspect of Cotswold barns can be easily fitted in to the foregoing chronology and historical developments. Indeed, it is impossible to give full justice to all of the various nuances and characteristics of the many hundreds of barns still to be found across the Cotswolds.

Some barns show a single distinctive element, others a relatively local characteristic. There are though a number of features which I feel merit additional consideration, and the following is simply an eclectic collection of interesting and curious ones which I have come across and which have particularly appealed to me.

They are collected under a variety of subsections, in no particular order or significance. It is quite possible that there are several other aspects which have eluded my many miles of travelling back and forth over the past few years. I can only say that I have thoroughly enjoyed every minute of roaming this delightful countryside and should anyone feel particularly slighted by any such omission I can only offer my apologies at this point, and request that you send the details to me. I will certainly endeavour to include these in any future illustrated talks or presentations. Equally it has been impossible to include all of the many hundreds of photographs which I have taken; consequently even my best efforts must remain selective at this point.

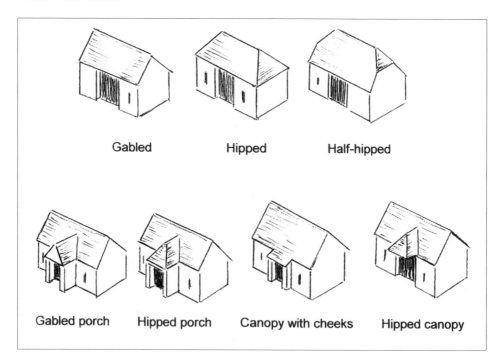

Gabled   Hipped   Half-hipped

Gabled porch   Hipped porch   Canopy with cheeks   Hipped canopy

108 Some typical barn and porch designs. *After Brunskill, 1982*

GABLES, PORCHES AND DOORS

As noted earlier in Chapter 3, gabled porches are a particularly characteristic feature of Cotswold barns. Indeed, porches are found from the earliest surviving medieval barns. A selection of the various types are presented in both schematic and pictorial form here (*108, 109* and *110*).

In larger barns, with a correspondingly substantial porch, a small door in the side of the porch can often be found (*111*). These, as already observed, would allow the farmer or granger to exit, having secured the main doors from inside. Larger cart entrances too would often have buttressed pillars. The large double doors were frequently hinged in sections to control the through draughts when winnowing, as noted earlier. It is, however, worth remembering when coming across a barn, whether still in use or redundant, to look out for evidence of where the threshing boards ('thresholds') might have been located (*112*).

Sometimes the space above these entrances was lofted and used as a granary, dovecote (*colour plate 19*) or as in the case of Bredon and Coxwell as accommodation, in which case it would be reached by either an external or internal staircase.

Above: 109 Double canopy and cheeks, Ewen

Below: 110 Gabled porches with additional protective lips over doors, near Barnsley

111 Side door used as final exit, after main doors are secured from the inside, Ablington

Left: 112 Slots for 'threshold' boards below old doors, Coates (before recent conversion)

Opposite above: 113 Outside stone steps to lofted area, Doughton

Opposite below: 114 Stone steps to barns at Duntisbourne Leer

OUTSIDE STAIRCASES

External short flights of steps are especially common as entrances to a hay loft, particularly in small barns which may have had a floor added at a later date when accommodating animals (*113, 114* and *colour plate 20*). These frequently add to the inherent attractiveness of such buildings.

115 Various provisions for animal housing, Middle Duntisbourne

116 Shelter sheds, Stanton Harcourt

OTHER RELATED BUILDINGS

On a typical mixed farm, provision would have been made for cattle, horses, sheep and pigs depending on the relative arable/pastoral emphasis of the area or individual farm (*115*). Shelter sheds are frequently found on one side of the yard, open-fronted and with solid end walls, the roof generally supported on stone piers (*116, colour plate 16*). From the mid-nineteenth century such shelter sheds were also added to a number of field barns, thus acting as a 'satellite' farm.

The large monastic granges or manorial farms would frequently have a separate granary; such a building was not really necessary on smaller farms until crop yields increased significantly when the need for more specialised storage became apparent (see *90*). This structure also had the advantage of allowing the farmer to keep his crop until he could obtain a better price.

Left: 117 Potence, for collecting eggs from nest holes in circular dovecote

Above: 118 Four-gabled, square dovecote with lantern on top, Naunton

DOVECOTES

These specially built houses for keeping domestic pigeons, variously known as dovecotes, columbaria and culverhouses (the latter from the Anglo-Saxon, *culver*, for pigeon), were a key source of food supplement in the Middle Ages as discussed in the previous chapter.

One of the earliest remaining examples of circular dovecotes can be found at Quenington in Gloucestershire (see *83*). The walls are 1.2m thick, with two widely splayed slit windows and it is believed to date from the thirteenth century, standing on a site that belonged to the Knights Hospitaller. A working potence is still in situ (*117*). This is a central wooden pole, pivoted above and below, which is attached to a ladder by means of lateral arms, thus allowing easy access to the tiers of nest boxes around the walls as it is rotated. Other round dovecotes can be seen in Daglingworth; the one in the grounds of the manor also has its potence providing access to some 550 nest holes in this case.

A cupola, or lantern, was often built on the top to provide both an entrance for the birds and protection against the elements. Some owners installed dormer windows to provide additional light and ventilation, and even windows in the sides.

119 Six-gabled, two-chambered dovecote, Lower Slaughter

Four-gabled, square, stone buildings are a characteristic feature of many Cotswold dovecotes. Typical examples are those at Fiddington Manor (with a date plaque of 1637), Carswell Manor andNaunton by the river Windrush (*118*). A fine square dovecote can also be seen in the car park of the village pub at Wytham. Somewhat more unusual is the larger six-gabled, two-chambered stone dovecote at what was formerly Lower Slaughter Manor (*119*), and a rather ornate one stands in a meadow across from Chastleton House; this has an upper-storey pigeon loft and an open arcaded ground floor.

During the seventeenth and eighteenth centuries the square and rectangular plan gradually disappeared in favour of an octagonal and occasionally a hexagonal design. Some 500 nesting holes can be found in the eighteenth-century octagonal dovecote at Frampton Court and, as with one at Painswick, it too is built with ashlar stone; the latter has a square arcaded summer house below. Perhaps the most unique is the columbarium in the church at Elkstone (*120*). This is above the chancel and is reached by a newel stairway behind the pulpit.

120 Columbarium above chancel, Elkstone church

ADORNMENTS

Finials
Commonly seen on even quite humble houses throughout the Cotswolds, and frequently on barns too, are a variety of decorative finials. These add a focal point and flourish to many gable peaks. Most widespread are variations on a simple ball shape (*121, 122*). Church Farm at Westwell has a ball on a square pedestal on each of the gable ends and porch of its main barn and a curious mid-roof adornment on the ridge (*123, colour plate 5*), with variations on the outbuildings. More ornate ones (as we have seen in Chapter 4) can be found at Middle Littleton, Stanway and Bradford-on-Avon.

Carvings
Carvings are far less frequent, but nevertheless bring a unique individuality to the area. Westwell seems quite unique in that it has a variety of carvings on and around the gable end of the porch; these include a man's head, several rather abstract swirls, an ammonite and a very weathered animal head (*124, 125*). One suggestion made is that these were simply Jacobean embellishments. At Southrop there is a splendid carving above the arch of the *c.*1847 ox-house and at Postlip

121 Ball finials on barns near Turksdean

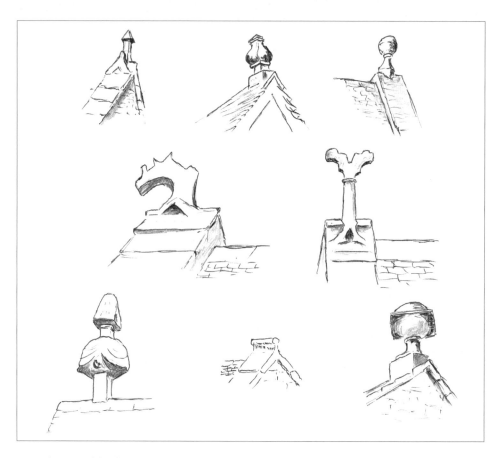

122 Selection of finials on barns across the Cotswolds

123 Mid-roof adornment on barn at Westwell

124 Gable end with carvings, Church Farm, Westwell

125 Weathered animal head and ammonite, Westwell

126 Carvings above ox-house, Southrop and above tithe barn at Postlip

on the west gable end of the circa fifteenth-century tithe barn the rather curious small squat figure of what is claimed to be Sir Richard de Postlip (*126*). The latter is mounted on a very typical small carved top to the capping stones.

OTHER UNIQUE OR UNUSUAL FEATURES

In Eynsham at Blankstones Farm is, from the outside, a typical small Cotswold stone barn – and yet from the inside it is entirely lined with red brick. This is obviously an intentional aspect of the construction as it not simply a piecemeal bit of infilling or repair when no stone was conveniently at hand, as may often to be found in other situations (*127*).

On a barn at Yarnton and a long byre at Westwell shingle roofs appear to have replaced the more typical stone slates (*128*). These are obviously much lighter and may have been considered as a viable alternative to undertaking considerable reconstructive work where a wall had begun to bow.

127 Brick-lined stone barn, Blankstones Farm, Eynsham

128 Shingle roof on byre at Westwell

'THEN AND NOW' EXAMPLES

Interesting too, especially from a conservation perspective, are some past and present comparisons of specific barns in their immediate context. These are often interesting both from an historical perspective and from a current design point of view; an issue to which we will return in more detail in the next chapter.

Price's Barn at Southrop has retained almost all of its major external features, such as the dovecote built into the gable ends as well as the front elevation of the building, producing a very pleasing effect: the only break in the line of the roof comes from the addition of a stone chimney (*129*, *130*). This was first converted in 1974 and then underwent further substantial internal changes in 1972 under the direction of the architect Peter Yiangou.

In Winson, a village of several converted barns, it is just possible to make out the location of an earlier delightful rural scene. The particular conversion illustrated is somewhat less sympathetic to the original structure, though obviously limited by the much smaller initial size of the byre (*131*, *132*). Nevertheless, simpler less fussy windows might have been considered as it seems unlikely that the current ones would receive present-day planning approval.

129 Price's Barn, Southrop, before conversion

130 Price's Barn, Southrop, after conversion

Left: 131 Rural scene at Winson.
Courtesy Museum of English Rural Life, Reading

Below: 132 Present-day conversion at Winson

133 Barns at Coates before recent conversion

134 Sett's Barn, Coates, after conversion

A recent conversion at Sett's Barn, Coates, has achieved a harmonious blend with modern materials and careful pointing. The external walls have only been minimally breached, yet light floods into the open, full-height main living area from the well set back windows in the large gabled porch (*133, 134, colour plates 21, 22*).

7

MODERN USAGES

The potential conflict between conservation and conversion to other uses is perhaps nowhere more clearly seen than in the issues surrounding the development of barns for alternative purposes. Despite this understandable concern, the conversion of redundant barns for either domestic or other commercial uses is something which has to be addressed. One cannot expect farmers to take on the responsibility and costs of maintaining and preserving buildings which have little or no use in a modern agricultural economy. Working efficiently with obsolete buildings is equivalent to expecting the manufacturer to work efficiently with outdated plant. On the other hand, historic farm buildings are by far the most numerous types of historic structures in the countryside, from the huge medieval estate and tithe barns to the lowlier field barns which dot the wolds; they form an essential record of both our agricultural history and vernacular architecture. They are also forming part of the historic landscape which is increasingly becoming a tourist commodity.

Neither of course, as we have already seen, can or should they be viewed in a static fashion. Over the centuries they have been replaced, or modified and adapted to meet the changing needs of evolving farm practices. Some, as shown, have undergone several modifications. It is, however, the unprecedented rate of change over the past 60 or so years that has led to the accelerated rate of redundancy and decay of so many of these buildings. In addition, the many conversions in the past two decades may not only be destroying irreplaceable evidence but also impacting on the very quality of our valued landscape. The issue then becomes the extent to which these different demands can be reconciled, as only a small population of these buildings can be afforded protection by national agencies and preserved as they stand.

Quantifying the rate of loss or disappearance of these assets is by no means an easy task. Charles and Horn, writing in 1983, expressed their concern over the endangered nature of surviving medieval barns – not least of all from the inherent risk of fire due to the material in their (timber) roofs and the vulnerable stacks of straw and hay which they sheltered. Of a dozen such medieval barns they had visited and surveyed since 1960, four had already perished in fires (including Bredon; see Chapter 4). They also reported estimates of sixteenth- and seventeenth-century redundant barns, which at that time had not 'attracted the attention of even the student of vernacular architecture' disappearing at the rate of one every week across the country as a whole.[10] They considered accurate estimation of this was impossible, as farmers who were in sole control of their barns were not prone to seeking permission to demolish a building which they no longer needed and which had become an economic liability.

Over 20 years ago the Society for the Protection of Ancient Buildings (SPAB) as a first principle argued for the retention of agricultural usage for such barns, even if this required conversion. This is because it was considered that alterations needed to keep the barn within farming use would have considerably less impact on architecture than those needed if the barns were to be used for other purposes. Nevertheless, the Society was perfectly cognisant of the fact that this could not always be the case and changes for other uses (given certain guidelines) may well be preferable to simply letting a barn or similar building fall into disrepair and ultimately complete ruin and loss. Where the retention of a barn could only be ensured by a change of use, then the SPAB considered that various factors should be taken into account and that certain classes of conversion were potentially more suitable than others. They were essentially those which respected the scale, space and architectural character of the building in question.

At the time of writing the issue is receiving considerable national attention as English Heritage has just published its fourth annual survey of England's historic environment, identifying principal trends affecting this environment together with the threats and challenges faced.[11] Amongst the issues, the condition of the historic farm building stock is considered in great detail. The decline in profitability of agriculture, as already noted, presents important challenges and pressures on these traditional buildings. The survey assessed patterns of neglect, decay and conversion in the listed farm building stock. Of the more than 30,000 listed working farm buildings (i.e. excluding farmhouses) about a third have already been converted to other uses, mainly residential. In the more remote areas they are often facing dereliction. In fact 7.4 per cent of listed buildings are in the severest state of repair, with the west midlands having the highest proportion of buildings with structural failures. Little or no information appeared available for non-listed buildings, though Defra's 2004 Farm Practices Survey identified significant and widespread levels of disrepair amongst working buildings on the farmstead. The greatest pressures were for conversion of listed buildings into dwellings, with much lower demands for conversion for alternative economic reuse. The Cotswolds were by no means the only area under pressure, though they did have one of the highest proportions of farm buildings converted to alternative uses.

In conjunction with the above survey and following on from the 2002 conference on sustainability, sponsored by the Countryside Agency and English Heritage, Gaskell and Owen (2005) have produced an important monograph which is seen as a first step towards addressing the gap in information regarding the size, character, condition and trajectory of change affecting traditional farm buildings resulting from the restructuring of the farming industry and other processes in the countryside. They also view farm buildings as integral to the agricultural landscape. Consequently they should be considered as a cultural and economic resource; and as such, one that is under threat. The authors distinguish between two types of loss. Absolute loss through demolition or neglect and relative loss resulting from loss of character due to unsuitable repairs or change of use which damages the historic character of the building.

Certainly in the context of the Cotswolds, the characteristic threshing barn has a number of architectural and spatial features which any type of conversion should attempt to respect. Specifically features like the pitch and sweep of the roof, the simplicity of the exterior with few openings, apart from the cart entrances and porches, the quality of the traditional materials and the internal timber framed structure. While recognising that every case is different, certain broadly defined principles can be considered when viewing the various types of conversion which have been undertaken.

COMMUNITY USE

Barns can be relatively easily adapted into places of assembly and used as village halls with a minimal loss of character; we have already noted one or two fine examples within the region, namely those at Stanway and Church Enstone. Others similarly have been successfully converted to community use as local theatres and have retained many of their original characteristics. At Bretforten, the early medieval barn built for the Abbey of Evesham has been converted into a successful theatre. This is largely built of local stone with some timber cladding (presumably added at a later date as this was little used before 1500) and is now under a red tile roof. A smaller but attractive and little-altered barn next to the church at Eastleach Martin is used for local and family occasions, particularly for a candle-light 'get-together' following the annual carol service (*135*). The tithe barn on the edge of Bourton-on-the-Hill has been completely refurbished inside to provide a restaurant, exhibition area and delightful setting for concerts. It has seven bays and substantial gabled porches on both its north and south sides. Above the north porch is a date-stone showing 1570 with the initials RP; for Richard Palmer, the man who had it built (*136*). The entire barn is built in a warm ashlar stone and appears very little altered from the outside.

Some have extended their social functions to providing a facility for wedding receptions, particularly some of the old tithe barns which remain in private hands. Adaptations have also been made for conference and educational uses. Here, relatively small internal structural changes and additions may be required, again making good use of the internal space, with the indigenous materials being retained as intrinsic features.

A few have managed to be retained almost in their original capacity, either as a working museum, as for example at Cogges, near Witney, or as a repository for historical farm machinery as at Swalcliffe.

135 Carefully maintained barn used for family and social occasions at Eastleach Martin

136 Tithe Barn, Bourton-on-the-Hill, used for social and cultural purposes

HOLIDAY USE

With the recent trends in diversification encouraged by various government agencies, a number of farmers have converted their barns, and particularly the various outbuildings, into holiday cottages and accommodation. The latter have often been modelled on the successful gîtes seen throughout France. While this provides a good use of otherwise redundant buildings, it often leaves them less recognisable in terms of their original use since building regulations for such accommodation may tend to make demands which are somewhat incompatible with the original design: a good example is to be found at Bruern.

As yet, there seems little, if any evidence, of field barns being used for basic overnight accommodation ('stone tents') as is increasingly common in the wilder areas of Derbyshire or Yorkshire – but this is much more to do with the lack of open spaces and uncultivated areas of the Cotswolds compared with moorland areas, and so is unlikely to occur.

LIGHT INDUSTRY AND CRAFTS

Various light industrial and manufacturing processes can also be carried on in barns and farm buildings as they, too, may be less likely to interrupt the essential

137 Barns and farm building converted for commercial offices, near Great Barrington

form of the building. They may be particularly compatible with both the spatial and functional qualities of the barn and often require minimal external alterations. The Cotswold District Council has in fact produced a useful guide which includes a section entitled 'Conversion of Historic Farm Buildings: to employment use'. This pamphlet also provides an artist's impression of a typical 'converted' historic farmstead. Delivery and access can frequently be accommodated satisfactorily via the porch entrances and a number of interesting examples exist, especially where a group of previously redundant barns and related buildings have been concerned.

A small group of barns and farm buildings near Great Barrington, one with a date-stone of 1879, provide quite a good example of such a commercial conversion (*137*). Similar examples are increasingly to be found throughout the Cotswolds. Also, established some time ago were the CoSIRA (Council for Small Industries in Rural Areas) workshops at Coalyard Farm, Northleach.

Successful conversions into centres for arts and crafts are also to be found throughout the region. At Filkins, for example, a group of traditional farm buildings, together with a splendid threshing barn, have been converted to use as various craft workshops, an exhibition gallery and shop. Built in 1721 the barn, formerly known as Bridal Barn, now houses the Cotswold Woollen Weavers (*138*, *colour plate 24*).

138 Farm buildings converted for use as craft workshops, Filkins

OTHER COMMERCIAL USES

It is also not uncommon to see barns which have been converted into restaurants, as for example the Carvery on the A40 between Witney and Burford; even a Little Chef at Burford retains many of the external tiers of nestholes provided for previous residents of this barn (*139, 140*). Other aspects of the building leave little indication as to its original use and design.

Several of the larger barns with adjoining outbuildings, and which form part of the larger farmyard, are used as riding stables. At Siddington (see also Chapter 4) these are partly housed in the impressive thirteenth-century, five-bay, mixed cruck and aisled barn and an attached smaller late eighteenth-century barn which have changed relatively little over the years. Busy riding stables can also be found housed in a splendid set of barns at Poultmoor Farm near Barnsley and at Ablington.

At Southrop, the former nineteenth-century ox-house (see *89*) has recently been exceptionally well converted into modern livery stabling with integral accommodation and office facilities (*141*). The adjacent large seventeenth-century barn is also being converted for commercial letting. These buildings were previously part of the manor, bought by Dorothy Wadham in 1612 and presented to her husband's foundation, Wadham College in Oxford, with whom it remained until sold by the college in 1926. In the same village another barn is being used by a

139 Carvery Restaurant, between Witney and Burford

140 Little Chef, near Burford, retaining some details of former occupants

141 Modern livery and accommodation in previous ox-house, Southrop

142 Commercial offices in converted barn, Southrop

financial company (*142*). The protective lip over the original cart entrance has been retained, as have the external stairs to earlier lofts. At White Hill, near Burford, the farm and barn, with an 1833 date-stone, are now used as a garden nursery (see *51*).

Beyond the conversion principles already outlined, the scope is often only limited by cost, the imagination of the architect and the need to find builders with the skills to use traditional materials.

DOMESTIC HOUSING

Despite a strong preference shown by various agencies for employment-related use, there can be little doubt that the greatest pressure is to be found on the conversion of redundant barns for domestic housing. It is in this category that the greatest emotions and conflicts of interest are often aroused. This is especially true when so-called conversions are literally turned into newly built houses, often only having gained planning consent due to the precedent set by the existing building, and showing virtually no resemblance whatsoever to the original building and its particular features. If it is a conventional modern house an individual seeks, then a barn conversion is not for them. Kate Corbett-Winder (1990) has produced a splendid book illustrating the sense of adventure that can be gained from living in a barn conversion. Her travels across the country identifying barns, stables and granaries, all empty and threatened by the growth and scale of modern farming and which have been restored, shows what can be achieved. A number of her examples include building in the Cotswolds.

There is little doubt that converting barns in a sensitive manner and retaining the essential characteristics of the original building can be quite difficult and certainly is not a cheap option. Once windows, doors and chimneys are introduced, to say nothing of satellite dishes and TV aerials or service connections, the simple austere character can easily be destroyed. A variety of other related issues have also been discussed by a number of authorities. Nevertheless, if the choice is between conversion and ruin then Hughes (1985) has outlined a number of guidelines and principles which, if followed as far as possible, will help keep any loss of character to a minimum.

Maintaining the sense of space and simplicity is perhaps the best starting point. This will generally involve the central threshing area, and if a single space can be retained, up to the full height of the roof, then so much the better. In fact, it is the roof itself which usually has such a dominant effect on the scale and character of the interior that demands it be a key feature within the design. If a living space from ground to ridge is not feasible, then an upper galleried area may provide a practical solution. Smaller, cosy rooms can often be provided at one end, especially when an attached byre or shelter shed can be incorporated into the conversion. A variety of imaginative uses can be made of the large threshing door openings, particularly in terms of providing a substantial body of light to the interior. This has been achieved in quite a successful way at Sett's Barn in Coates, where the sense of height and space has been utilised to good advantage. In addition, continuity has been gained by the use of stone flooring from the inside to the outside in each of the cart entrances: this openness also allows maximum advantage to be gained from an evening sunset across the open-field vista (*colour plate 25*).

Other windows need to be as discreet as possible. Ventilation slits can often be incorporated in such a way, and if facing outward towards a public road may help to provide both privacy and a simple exterior. It is often helpful too if symmetry can be avoided when adding additional windows. Extra daylight might be achieved by the use of skylights, especially if they can be used in a discrete and unobtrusive position. They also have the benefit of retaining the original sweep of the roof, though small dormers can be quite in keeping with other Cotswold characteristics.

Retaining as much as possible of the original fabric adds to the charm and character of the inside of the building too, particularly the old beams and rafters which often have unusual shapes and configurations. Except for building regulations which will require plastering in bathrooms, it is also preferable to keep as much of the exposed stonework as possible. This undecorated quality is not only in keeping with the original building's material but also has the benefit of being low maintenance. It can not only provide an attractive feature, but on ground level rooms it can also help obviate any possible problems of damp appearing on plastered areas as it can be very difficult to provide an entirely adequate damp coursing to these buildings. In fact it can offer a very satisfactory built-in humidifier to the otherwise dry climate produced by modern central heating.

An important aspect often easily overlooked, is the very setting itself. Achieving a harmony with the surroundings can make an enormous difference to the appearance of a converted barn. Nothing destroys the simplicity more than fussy fencing, inappropriate planting, harsh surfaces and ill-conceived garaging. Adaptation may sometimes be less than ideal, but suburbanisation of the countryside can only lead to a significant and irrevocable loss.

Clearly if such changes are to be undertaken, a concerted joint collaboration throughout the entire process is required between good planning guidance, a knowledgeable architect and a sympathetic owner, together with an emphasis on local materials and traditional methods. Given all of these limitations and considerations a number of very good examples can be found throughout the Cotswolds. One or two are outlined below by way of illustration, but are by no means exhaustive or comprehensive as the numbers are being added to almost on a weekly basis.

A simple but elegant conversion of a small barn, which has retained the essential feel of the internal and external structure, can be seen in Harvey's Barn in Fifield (143, 144). A similar example of a conversion, keeping the simple lines of the original barn and retaining the uncomplicated farmyard feel, is the nearby mid-eighteenth-century barn at Hill Farm (near Bruern). Half of the barn is still in use for stabling and the opposite half has been converted for domestic use and is linked to the adjoining farmhouse. Both aspects are accessed unobtrusively via the retained central cart entrance. The external fabric has been sensitively renovated and carefully repointed using lime mortar (145, 146). A similar example of a conversion, keeping the simple lines of the original barn, retaining the uncomplicated farmyard feel and using a row of five small windows tucked under the eaves (rather than roof lights), contributes to a successful design illustrated in Hill and Birch's (1994) book (see case study no. 6).

Leighterton is a village where the County Council owned a number of farms within the village confines, and which applied in 1986 to convert these to residential use. They are all grouped in a relatively small area, several retaining their original date-stones and most are still quite recognisable (147), as is a large barn at Kemble (148).

Finally, two other barns, one at Ascott-under-Wychwood and the other at Winson are presented. These are included simply as being illustrative of some of the variations in barn design and the scope which such buildings offer; they are not intended as model representations (149, 150).

143 Harvey's Barn, Fifield

144 Interior view, Harvey's Barn

145 Hill Farm Barn, near Bruern: half converted to domestic use, half used as stabling

Left: 146 Stabling at Hill Farm Barn

Middle and below: 147 Before and after views of 1806 barn at Leighterton

Oppsoite above and middle: 148 Old and recent views of large barn at Kemble

Opposite below: 149 Converted barn and shelter sheds at Ascott-under-Wychwood

150 Converted barn, Winson

Adhering to the essential principles discussed, one can certainly see the attraction for many of living in such a building, keeping alive a fabric which is so much part of our cultural heritage.

William Morris, the founder of SPAB, said that he 'would like a house like a big barn, where one ate in one corner, cooked in another corner, slept in the third corner and in the fourth received ones friends'. This is understandable, and still being achieved by a number of people.

NOTES

CHAPTER 1 THE COTSWOLDS

1 Sturge Gretton 1914
2 Sutton, A. & Hudson, J. 1988
3 Fowler, P. 1982

CHAPTER 2 REGIONAL CHARACTERISTICS

4 Sturge Gretton 1914 *Op. Cit.*
5 Personal communication, Arthur Price of Frocester Court

CHAPTER 3 GENERAL CONSTRUCTION

6 Munby, J.T. & Steane, J.M. 1995
7 Dyer, C. in Charles, F.W.B. 1997

CHAPTER 4 EARLY MEDIEVAL ESTATE AND TITHE BARNS

8 Dyer, C. 1997 *Ibid.*

CHAPTER 5 HISTORICAL DEVELOPMENTS AND CHANGING PATTERNS OF USE

9 Copland, S. 1866

CHAPTER 7 MODERN USAGES

10 Charles, F.W.B. & Horn, M. 1983 p214
11 Cowell, B., Trow, S. & Tunnicliffe, S. Eds. 2005

GLOSSARY

ASHLAR — masonry with even face and square edges

BAY — space formed by vertical posts, buttresses or roof beams along a barn interior (usually between 8ft and 16ft long)

BOX FRAME — skeleton frame, usually wood with various in-fill materials

BRACE — subsidiary timber support; e.g. wind-brace in plane of roof; sling-brace between wall post and rafter

BYRE — cowshed

COLLAR — horizontal beam, above and parallel to the main tiebeam, joining two sides of roof running between and tying together the sloping rafters

CRUCK BLADES — timber beams carrying the main weight, usually curved, and in pairs cut from the same tree, sloping inwards and joined at the top forming an inverted 'V' or rough arch. May have their feet at ground level: *base cruck,* blades rise from ground level to a tiebeam or collar; *full cruck,* blades rise from ground level to apex of roof part way up the wall; *raised cruck* or may rise from a tiebeam; *jointed cruck* where the blade is made from two timbers joined together

DRESSED STONE — worked to a decorative finish

FINIAL — topmost feature of gable roof or canopy, generally ornamental

FLAIL — tool for threshing; made of a wooden staff and stouter end piece (a swingle or swipple) and connected together by leather or tough skin

FREESTONE — blocks of stone for carving and making mullion windows etc. and 'free' of fossils found in much of the Cotswolds

COTSWOLD BARNS

GABLE	the wall at the end of a ridged roof, usually triangular
HIPPED ROOF	see drawings of typical barn porch shapes, p.118
JOWL	thickening of post at its top
KING POST	central post rising from tiebeam to ridge
LANTERN	small turret with openings or windows all around, often used as access for pigeons on a barn or dovecote
MIDSTREY	door or porch opening onto threshing floor
OWL HOLES	round, triangular or elongated holes high up in the gable end to attract owls as a means of vermin control
PENDLE	naturally occurring fissile material; stone left out in the open for frost to split before being made into slates
PLINTH	projecting base of a wall or column
POST AND TRUSS	building method where the roof load is supported by internal vertical posts and horizontal trusses, rather than by the wall itself
PRESENTS	slates/tiles which come direct from the quarry and which splits naturally into layers or thin slabs ready for making up and which do not have to be left out over winter to be split by frost (as with the Stonesfield Slates)
PRINCIPAL RAFTERS	rafter of large section normally associated with tiebeams. The remaining rafters are *common rafters*
PURLINS	longitudinal timbers supporting rafters
PUTLOG HOLES	holes left from ends of scaffolding inserted into the wall as it goes up
QUEEN POSTS or STRUTS	two posts (or struts) supporting collar or principal rafter from tiebeam
QUOIN	a dressed stone at the external angle of a wall, often with small and large alternations
RIDGE	beam along top of roof
SCARF	a joint of two longitudinal timbers
SHINGLES	thin pieces of wood used for roofing, with parallel sides but with one end thicker than the other
TALLOT	loft over stables or above porch entrance to a barn
TIEBEAM	major transverse beam between main structural elements, usually at eaves level, tying together the feet of principal rafters to counteract outward thrust caused by weight of roof
TORCHING	filling in the spaces on the underside of slates or tiles with lime and hair mortar
WALL-PLATE	horizontal timber on top of wall to take and distribute the load from the rafters

BIBLIOGRAPHY

Aston, M. (1974) *Stonesfield Slate*. Oxfordshire Museum Services: publication No. 5

Bardswell, A. (1983) 'Sheltered by stone'. *Country Life* (Nov. 17th) Vol.174, No. 4500, pp.1474-75

Billet, M. (1979) *Thatching and Thatched Buildings*. Robert Hale

Binney, M. (1981) 'Renaissance of the barn'. *Country Life* (Jan. 22nd) pp.178-80

Bloemendal, F. & Hollingsworth, A. (1992) *Cotswold Architecture and Heritage*. Ian Allen Ltd, London

Brill, E. (1973) *Life and Tradition on the Cotswolds*. J.M. Dent, London

Brooks, J. (1994) 'The conflict between conservation and conversion: the residential re-use of barns'. *Unpublished PhD Thesis*. Oxford Brookes University

Brunskill, R.W. (1982) *Traditional Farm Buildings of Britain*. Victor Gollancz; Orion Group, London

Catto, J.I. & Evans, T.A.R. (1992) *The History of the University of Oxford*. Vol. II, Oxford University Press

Charles, F.W.B. (1997) *The Great Barn at Bredon: Its fire and reconstruction*. Oxbow Books

Charles, F.W.B. & Charles, M. (1984) *Conservation of Timber Buildings*. Donhead, Dorset

Charles, F.W.B. & Horn, W. (1983) 'The cruck-built barn of Frocester Court Farm, Gloucestershire'. *Journal of the Society of Architectural Historians, USA* Vol. XLII, pp.211-37

Clifton-Taylor, A. (1987) *The Pattern of English Building*. Faber & Faber, London

Copland, S. (1866) *Agriculture, Ancient and Modern*. Vol. 1

Corbett-Winder, K. (1990) *The Barn Book*. Ebury Press, London

Cowell, B., Trow, S. & Tunnicliffe, S. Eds. (2005) *Heritage Counts: the state of England's historic environment 2005*. English Heritage, London

Darley, G. (1988) *A Future for Farm Buildings*. Save Britain Heritage

Dyer, C. (1997) in Charles, F.W.B. *The Great Barn at Bredon*. Oxbow Books

Fay, J. & Martin, R. (1987) *The Jubilee Boy*. The Filkins Press, Lechlade

Finberg, J. (1997) *The Cotswolds*. Eyre Methuen, London

Gaskell, P. & Owen, S. (2005) *Historic Farm Buildings: Constructing the evidence base*. Countryside and Community Research Unit, University of Gloucestershire

Harris, R. (1989) 'The grammar of carpentry'. *Vernacular Architecture* Vol. 20, pp.1-8

Harvey, N. (1984) *A History of Farm Buildings in England and Wales*. David & Charles

Hill, M. & Birch, S. (1994) *Cotswold Stone Houses*. Sutton Publishing, Gloucestershire.

Hewett, C. (1982) in *The SPAB Barns Book*. Society for the Protection of Ancient Buildings, London

Horn, W. & Born, E. (1965) *The Barns of the Abbey of Beaulieu: Great Coxwell and Beaulieu St Leonards*. University of California Press

Horn, W. & Charles, F.W.B. (1966) 'The cruck-built barn of Middle Littleton in Worcestershire'. *Journal of the Society of Architectural Historians, USA* Vol.XXV, pp. 221-39

Hughes, G. (1985) *Barns of Rural Britain*. The Herbert Press, London

Kirk, M. (1994) *The Barn: silent spaces*. Thames & Hudson

Marshall, W. (1789) The Rural Economy of Gloucestershire. Vol.II

Massingham, H.J. (1937) *Cotswold Country*. Batsford

Miles, A. (2003) *Cotswold Moods*. Halsgrove

Moriarty, D. (1989) *Buildings of the Cotswolds*. Victor Gollancz; Orion Group, London

Munby, J.T. & Steane, J.M. (1995) 'Swalcliffe: a New College Barn in the 15th Century'. *Oxoniensa LX*

Pearce, D. (1982) *The SPAB Barns Book*. Society for the Protection of Ancient Buildings, London

Peters, J.E.C. (1998) 'Barns in Gloucestershire'. *Vernacular Architecture* Vol. 29, pp.13-17

Pigram, R. & Edwards, D. (1996) *Cotswold Memories*. Greenwich

Sherwood, J. & Pevsner, N. (1974) *The Buildings of England: Oxfordshire*. Penguin

Steane, J.M. ed. (1978) *Cogges: A Museum of farming in the Oxfordshire Countryside*. Oxfordshire Museum Services

Sutton, A. & Hudson, J. (1988) *Cotswold Images*. Alan Sutton Publishing, Gloucestershire

Verey, D. & Brooks, A. (1999) *The Buildings of England: Gloucestershire 1; The Cotswolds*. Penguin

Wood-Jones, R. (1963) *Traditional Domestic Architecture of the Banbury Region*. Manchester University Press

INDEX

If you are interested in purchasing other books published by Tempus,
or in case you have difficulty finding any Tempus books in your local bookshop,
you can also place orders directly through our website

www.tempus-publishing.com